KW-112-768

Paternoster Pocket Book No. 27
My Chains Fell Off

'...To open eyes that are blind,
to free captives from prison
and to release from the dungeon
those who sit in darkness.'

Isaiah 42:7

Other books by Derek Copley
Home Bible Stories

With Nancy Copley
Shock Wave
Building with Bananas

My Chains Fell Off

Openness to God, ourselves
and others

by
Derek Copley
&
Mary Austin

Illustrated by
Bob Bond

EXETER:
THE PATERNOSTER PRESS

Copyright © 1982 Derek Copley & Mary Austin

All Rights Reserved. No part of this publication may be reproduced, stored in a
retrieval system, or transmitted, in any form or by any means, electronic,
mechanical, photocopying, recording or otherwise, without the prior permission of
THE PATERNOSTER PRESS

AUSTRALIA:
Bookhouse Australia Ltd.,
P.O. Box 115,
Flemington Markets, NSW 2129

SOUTH AFRICA:
Oxford University Press, P.O. Box 1141, Cape Town

This book is sold subject to the condition that it shall not, by way of trade or otherwise, be lent,
re-sold, hired out, or otherwise circulated without the publisher's prior consent in any form of
binding or cover other than that in which it is published and without a similar condition
including this condition being imposed on the subsequent purchaser.

British Library Cataloguing in Publication Data

Copley, Derek Bryan
    My chains fell off. – (Paternoster pocket books : 27)
    1. Christian life
    I. Title   II. Austin, Mary
    248.4   BV4501.2

ISBN 0-85364-314-8

*Typeset by Photo-Graphics, Honiton, Devon and printed in Great Britain by Butler and
Tanner Ltd., Frome, Somerset for The Paternoster Press Ltd., Paternoster House, 3
Mount Radford Crescent, Exeter, Devon.*

Contents

Acknowledgements

Biblical quotations (unless otherwise stated) are from the New International Version published by Hodder & Stoughton, copyright 1978 by the New York International Bible Society.

Graham Kendrick's song *My True Feelings* (copyright © 1976/G. Kendrick/Thankyou Music), extracts are used by kind permission.

Material from *The Princess and the Frog* is reproduced from the Ladybird book *The Princess and the Frog* by Vera Southgate, published by Ladybird Books Ltd., Loughborough, with the permission of the publishers.

'May I Introduce You To A Friend' is from *Come Together* by Jimmy & Carol Owens, © copyright 1972 Lexicon Music Inc., used by permission. All rights reserved.

We would also like to acknowledge the patient help of Lorraine Groves who typed the manuscript.

Dedicated to
Nancy Copley
and Mary's parents
Clifford and Myrtle Austin
and her sister Linda

Preface

When something great happens in your life, your natural desire is to share it with other people. So when God touched and transformed our relationships with him, we found we wanted to tell everyone about it. 'What better way of doing this than through a book?' we thought. And so we began to pray about the idea to see if God was behind it.

The odds against our working together on this project were huge. How could God ever dream of bringing together two people like us? It seemed impossible. One of us was a married Bible College Principal with a non-charismatic background and twenty years' Christian experience behind him. The other was a single female college student who had become a charismatic at her conversion less than five years previously.

At first we were doubtful whether or not to begin the manuscript. We even delayed working on it for five months to make sure that we were hearing God right! Perhaps we just coudn't believe that this kind of co-authorship was possible. Yet all the time God seemed to be leading us to write jointly.

Then the specific guidance came. Independently each of us was confronted by Bible verses about authorship: 'Go now, write it on a tablet for them, inscribe it on a scroll, that for the days to come it may be an everlasting witness' (Isaiah 30:8). 'This is what the Lord, the God of Israel, says: Write in a book all the words I have spoken to you' (Jeremiah 30:2). 'Write down the revelation and make it plain on tablets' (Habakkuk 2:2). After this we didn't feel we had much choice!

Right from the start we had our problems. Working with someone who has a totally different character from yours isn't at all easy. Emotionally, we were complete opposites—one strong and independent, the other sensitive and dependent. When we added together all the differences between us, we agreed it would be a miracle if we ever managed to produce anything at all!

But as we began writing, we soon realised why God had brought us together. It was the very differences in our lives that formed the key to the whole book. In a remarkable way we represented between us just about every kind of Christian there could ever be: male, female, married, single, long-standing Christian, recent convert 'non-charismatic' background, 'charismatic' from the beginning, strong/independent and sensitive/dependent. Everyone could identify with us in some way.

What we also saw was that our relationship as authors somehow proved it was possible for people with completely opposite characteristics to get on together. At times we really had to work hard to maintain harmony between us. We were reminded of the Church, the body of Christ, and of how people of all sorts of persuasions meet to worship and serve God. They can live in harmony—if they want to and are prepared to work at it. (Derek and Nancy Copley have already written about that in *Building with Bananas*.

We hope that those who read this book will find it rewarding. We'd like it to challenge individuals to open up their lives to God and others. We'd like it to challenge whole churches to get together to take an honest look at where they're going. But whether it is read alone, or studied in groups, we thought that the 'points to ponder' would be helpful guidelines. Some of the points are probably better for personal use only and groups may wish to avoid these. We'll leave you to decide.

This book is not complete and it never will be. It's the story of what has happened so far in the lives of two ordinary Christians. It shows how God has released us from all sorts of bondage and given us new freedom in Christ. God is still working on us, and we hope our experience will be shared by our readers.

In particular, we hope that many will find new meaning in Charles Wesley's words:

My chains fell off, my heart was free,
I rose, went forth, and followed Thee.

"...LIVING OUT OUR CHRISTIANITY LIKE MISERABLE PRISONERS IN A HUGE DARK DUNGEON."

Freedom for the Prisoners

Name: Copley, Derek Bryan
Place of Birth: Accrington, Lancashire, England
Date of Birth: 9th August 1940
Married/Single: Married
Wife's Name: Nancy Harrell
Wife's nationality: American
Children: Two—David Martin, Sarah Elizabeth
Occupation: Principal, Moorlands Bible College
Converted: 1st October 1958
Church Background: Open Brethren
Character: Sensitive, dependent

Name: Austin, Mary Jennifer
Place of Birth: London, England
Date of Birth: 30th April 1954
Married/Single: Single
Occupation: Nothing stable yet (trained in hotel and
    catering)
Converted: 20th October 1974
Church Background: United Reformed then Open
    Brethren
Character: Strong, independent

Statistical summaries of people never tell you very much, but they do give you some idea of who individuals are. You may never have heard of us before. We're just two Christians among millions. We're not special Christians but ordinary ones—like you, in fact!

You'd be able to make a list of your own characteristics as we have, but it would be very different from either of ours although parts might be similar or even identical. But you'd never be able to copy precisely the same skeleton picture for yourself. That's because you're unique. You may think you're the most insignificant Christian in the world but you're unique to God. He loves you and he wants you to discover how important you are to him as he shows you his plan for your life.

What are you like?

What do you look like physically? Fat? Thin? Tall? Short? Muscular? Spindly? Beautiful? Spotty? Do you realise that God has accepted you just as you are? You might not be satisfied with your appearance but he loves you no matter how you look. He rejoices over your life because he made you and he wants you to have a deeper relationship with him.

What do you 'look like' emotionally? Are you the sort of person who's strong and independent, someone who can manage things alone or are you rather insecure; do you tend to lean too heavily on others? Maybe you fall somewhere in between. It's good to know that God accepts and loves you regardless of the kind of person you are.

What do you 'look like' spiritually? Or is that a question you've never really thought too hard about? Maybe your Christian life seems just like that of other Christians with whom you meet every so often. You can speak about God's working in your life and you've been used to help others to come to Christ. 'What do you mean, what do I look like spiritually?' you may ask.

Well, put it this way: Do you know Jesus?

If you were asked about your relationship with Jesus,

what would you reply? For how long would you be able
to talk? Would you describe how you became a Christian
and then add a few general comments about how Jesus
helps you lead a good life? Would you answer with
phrases you've learnt from the Bible which you know
must be true? Or would you relate all the sensational
spiritual experiences you've had? You might even be
totally baffled about how to respond. But none of these
replies would really be answering the question: 'Do you
know Jesus?'

'But', you insist, 'of course I know him. I'm a Christian!' It's not quite as simple as that. You see, people who
claim to know Jesus well should be able to talk of him as
their personal friend. They'll hear him speaking directly
to them through his Word, the Bible, as they read it.
They'll also find that he talks to them through people and
everyday events. They'll know his voice and will learn to
follow him (John 10:4).

They'll be able to share their experience of worship and
of prayer and their knowledge that Jesus draws close and
listens. They'll relate answers to prayer—not just about
big things, but about little ones too. They'll lift all their
joys and sorrows to him and know that he'll always be
there beside them, sharing their laughter and their tears
(Matthew 28:20).

They'll long to speak of how he's been moving in their
lives and helping them to abandon the masks they put on
to hide their real selves from others. They'll be honest
about their weaknesses as well as their strengths and
they'll have joy because Jesus is steadily changing them
into his likeness (2 Corinthians 3:18).

They'll know what it's like to be freed as individuals
and won't want to be isolated believers. They'll want to
be involved, and to reach out and experience new joy in
relationships with other Christians. They'll love to help
people and, when in need themselves, they'll be happy to
allow others to help them. They'll open up their lives in
their fellowship, share their joys and sorrows, bear the
burdens of those who can't cope alone and discover how

to love and build up the body of Christ (Ephesians 4:16). So we ask once more—is yours a *real* relationship with Jesus?

Captivity—Ancient and Modern

The Pharisees in Jesus' time thought that they had a healthy relationship with God. 'The only Father we have is God himself' they declared (John 8:41). But Jesus accused them of being children of the devil (8:44) and of being blind (9:41). He told them that they needed to be set free, but they wouldn't believe that they were slaves to a system of petty rules and regulations. 'We are Abraham's descendants and have never been slaves of anyone. How can you say that we shall be set free' (8:33)?

Exactly the same thing happens with Christians today. 'We're not restricted,' we declare. And then we try to prove it. 'Our fellowship has been doing great things for the Lord and he's really been blessing us spiritually. Look how our numbers have increased!' We refuse to believe that we could actually be in chains and might not be enjoying a satisfying relationship with God at all.

There are too many active and even 'Spirit-filled' Christians who claim to enjoy the closeness of God but who don't. They 'do things' for him, they may experience his power, but they don't know him intimately. He's about as real to them as the man in the moon! Like the Pharisees, they're blinded and bound by their assertion: 'We have a strong relationship with God', when they've hardly got one at all. They say Christianity is a joyful faith, but they walk around with long faces. They declare: 'The Bible is the Word of God', but they rarely read it, and it says nothing when they do. They maintain that God listens when they pray, but they seldom talk to him. They make out that Christian fellowship's great, but inwardly they aren't particularly interested in it, or they avoid close contact with others because they're afraid of being open about themselves. They rush into the meetings at the last minute and race away immediately they finish. That's just not true fellowship.

How many of us know these feelings too? Some of us are blinded by cold orthodoxy which states: 'You don't have to "experience" God; you just believe he's there (even if he doesn't seem to be). You work hard for him but you certainly don't get emotionally involved.' Others of us are blinded by spiritual experiences which lead us to believe that we've 'arrived', that 'baptism in the Spirit' is the key to our development, that our problems have come to an end.

In chains

It's really the devil who manages to convince us that we're on the right spiritual track when we're not. He delights to wind chains around us and padlock us into the sort of legalistic or over-emotional Christianity that will prevent us being a threat to him. Nothing delights him more than to see Christians treating the Word of God as a set of rules, worship and prayer as rituals, and relationships with other believers as non-essentials. He loves to see us hiding away our true feelings, deceiving ourselves that we're enjoying a relationship with God while we're living out our Christianity like miserable prisoners in a huge dark dungeon. And yet—Christ has set us free (Galatians 5:1).

In one sense, that is true of all of us. We've been delivered from the punishment for our sin through trusting him to save us (Acts 2:21). We now look forward to an eternal home in heaven (2 Peter 3:13).

But what about here on earth? Shouldn't we be living free and happy lives in God's service here too? Of course we should! The Bible makes it quite clear however that Christians can slip into bondage; otherwise Galatians 5:1 wouldn't continue with the words, 'Stand firm, then, and do not let yourselves be burdened again by a yoke of slavery.'

What I confidently describe as 'freedom in Christ' may not be freedom at all. I may have experienced only a very tiny amount of the liberty God longs for me to have.

The story is told of a man who went on a sea cruise. He took with him a large packet of sandwiches. On the first day of the trip he didn't go into the dining-room for his meals, but just began to eat the food he'd brought with him. On the second day he continued to eat his few remaining stale sandwiches. A puzzled fellow-passenger asked him why he didn't join everyone else for his meals. 'I couldn't afford it' came the reply. 'But' answered the fellow-passenger, 'your ticket entitles you to meals in the dining-room. The fare is all-inclusive!'

Jesus died to give us life 'to the full' (John 10:10), but too many Christians never really discover it. They're on board the ship bound for heaven but they prefer to live on their sandwiches rather than on the Bread of Life. God wants us to know the 'riches of his glorious inheritance in the saints, and his incomparably great power for us who believe' (Ephesians 1:18,19). He doesn't want us to be satisfied with anything less.

Seeking God for himself

We may want to have good times of Bible-study, praise, prayer and fellowship, to receive powerful spiritual revelations, to discover God's choice for a life-partner, to find his help with personal problems or happiness in our Christian lives. Our aim may be to be useful to people, or to work hard for God. All these are worth seeking but there's something even more important. It's summed up in Paul's statement: 'I want to know Christ' (Philippians 3:10).

The first and greatest command is that we love God (Matthew 22:37,38). True love cannot be found outside a relationship. Above all else, God wants us to enjoy a fulfilling relationship with himself, closely followed by a deep affection for our friends (22:39). The trouble is that too many of us today are seeking God for things and not for himself. We want his blessings or guidance or help more than we want an intimate friendship with him. So we remain unsatisfied because we're putting second things first. If we want to live our lives to the full, we've got to know where to go to fill them.

New life

Life is found in the person who didn't just claim to give it, but who embodies it. 'I am the…Life' (John 14:6). The more I know Jesus, the more I know what abundant life is all about. Out of a relationship with him will come all the blessings, guidance and help I could ever want. 'Delight yourself in the Lord and he will give you the desires of your heart' (Psalm 37:4). 'He who did not spare his own Son, but gave him up for us all—how will he not also, along with him, graciously give us all things?' (Romans 8:32).

At the beginning of this chapter we gave you a skeleton picture of ourselves but we didn't tell you what we looked like physically, emotionally or spiritually. We'll ignore the first of these because it's not really very important. What concerns God is not so much our physical but our spiritual appearance. That is often affected by our emotional condition. It was these two areas in our lives which caused us the most embarrassment.

It's amazing how easily you can hide your bad points from your friends! You can appear a dedicated, hard-working and successful Christian and yet be an emotional and spiritual wreck underneath.

We were like that—chained emotionally because we dared not be ourselves, and chained spiritually by rituals like 'Bible reading', 'praying' and 'having fellowship' which were done because we felt we ought to do them, not because we wanted to.

We might have succeeded in fooling men, but not an all-seeing God. He moved in and opened our eyes to the truth about ourselves. He showed us our chains and then, one by one, he broke them and set us free.

We're like two new people! Our whole relationship with God has been transformed and Scriptures like, 'If the Son sets you free, you will be free indeed' (John 8:36) now overflow with new meaning.

Points to Ponder

1. Many Christians see Christianity in terms of 'conversion and trying to live as God says'. Do you agree with this summary?

2. Before you read this chapter, did you think you knew Jesus well? Has reading it changed your opinion about your relationship with him?

3. How would you answer the following questions? Underline or tick the word that is nearest to the truth for you. (Remember to mark the way things are, not the way you would like them to be!)
   (a) God speaks to me through the Bible (often/sometimes/rarely/never)
   (b) God speaks to me in other ways, e.g. through people or events, (often/sometimes/rarely/never)
   (c) I speak to God (often/sometimes/rarely/never)
   (d) I am open with other people (very open/fairly open/rather closed/closed)
   (e) I consider close fellowship to be (vital/very important/important/quite important/not essential/a waste of time)

4. Consider your emotional life. Are you open and honest in this area with yourself, with God, with other people?

5. Do you think you personally can or should be emotionally involved with God? Or must your relationship with him remain rather distant and detached?

6. Are 'spiritual experiences' necessarily the answer to a person's need for a better relationship with Jesus?

7. Do you have any reservations about seeking the closeness to God described in this chapter?

"THAT ENTHUSIASTICALLY PRESENTED MESSAGE IS MET WITH BLANK EXPRESSIONS...."

2

The Bible—Dry and Dusty?
Derek

A good preacher spends a great deal of time preparing his sermons. He prays and studies hard until the message is just right for the occasion. Often, as a guest speaker, he has to travel long distances. Generally speaking he makes enormous personal sacrifices in order to bring God's word to the people and to lead them in worship.

When the day is over he usually ponders over how things have gone. Sometimes he feels disappointed at the 'deadness' in particular churches. The usual ten minute prayer meeting before the service seems to be nothing more than a dull routine. The hymns are sung so quietly that anyone with a normal voice would sound as though they were singing a solo. Few people respond to the prayers, and the Lord's Prayer is said as if the death penalty awaits anyone whose voice is raised above a whisper. The people seem so bored with it all.

What a speaker finds most distressing is the lack of response to his address. That enthusiastically presented message is met with blank expressions and occasional yawns. He isn't expecting every single person to be sitting on the edge of his seat throughout the sermon, or taking down on paper every word he utters—yet he does expect some evidence that people are listening to him, and what is more important, to God.

When the service is over, he'd love to see one or two staying behind to discuss something which has been a challenge or an encouragement. Often, there is nothing more than a series of polite smiles and handshakes at the door, with comments like, 'That was a lovely message, it must have spoken to the young people.'

Upset preacher—but how about God?

It's not just the preacher who suffers, it's God. The preacher may weep over yet another failure, but the pain felt by God is of a different order! God's sorrow is because many of his own people simply don't want to listen to what he's saying through his Word, the Bible.

This is just what happened in Old Testament times when God spoke to the Jews. Hosea writes movingly, 'The more I called Israel the further they went from me' (11:2). Jeremiah, feeling the anguish of a heart-broken God whose word had been rejected, wrote, 'My eyes will weep bitterly, overflowing with tears' (13:17) and 'Oh that my head were a spring of water and my eyes a fountain of tears! I would weep day and night' (9:1).

When Jesus knew that the Pharisees had finally decided not to listen to him, he wept over them (Luke 19:41). He must often weep today when Christians ignore his voice as they hear his Word being read and explained.

But Jesus doesn't give up. Like God in Hosea's day who said 'How can I give you up?' (11:8), Jesus keeps trying. Why? Because he loves his people and longs for them to respond joyfully to his voice.

Whose fault?

I'm the kind of person who blames himself when things go wrong. When a congregation sits lifeless during my sermon I often think, 'I can't have spent enough time in preparation.' Yet it isn't my fault every time!

So why don't people listen eagerly? I ask myself this question time and time again. Are congregations too familiar with the Bible and forget that it's *God*'s word to them? Has it become a book just for discussion and debate, without our personal involvement? Has the sermon become something we assess for its correctness, without allowing it to affect our lives?

Not all congregations are like this! In some churches people are eager to take in whatever God says. Even when I've told them not to bother to look up a particular verse, they still insist on doing so. Time doesn't seem to matter either. While most congregations become restless after just sixty minutes, others are still keen after two hours.

If we don't take much notice of the Bible in church it's probably because we have a poor relationship with it at home. If in private it has little impact on us, then it's hardly likely to affect us in a church service. Somewhere, somehow, many of us have not discovered the true purpose of God's Word in our daily lives, and until we do, church services will be hard going, because we won't have developed an expectancy that God will speak through the Scriptures.

Since I was concerned about people's personal relationship to the Word, I decided to ask a few people, 'What does the Bible mean to you?'

The replies showed that it was having very little effect on some Christians. Although they'd be too ashamed to admit it, a number found it to be boring and their relationship with it was dull and lifeless.

Here are some of the replies: 'I hate people who ask questions like this.'... 'Quite a bit.'... 'It's boring, and I get nothing out of it!'... 'It means nothing to me.'... 'It's the revelation of God to man today.' (Quite a good answer theologically, but it does not necessarily show personal involvement.)

Sharing the Word

When did you last share an exciting verse with someone?

'Who? Me? Well, er, um...' you might splutter in reply. 'I don't really know', might be another response. It's an embarrassing question because some of us can't really answer it.

Let me give you an example of what can happen when the Word of God starts to live. Some months ago I was sitting alone eating my cornflakes. Suddenly I felt such a burden for writing this book that I thought I was going to explode.

Shortly afterwards I had my time of reading and praying. I had been working through Job and on that particular day I came across a verse which really hit me: 'Inside I am like bottled-up wine, like new wineskins ready to burst. I must speak and find relief' (Job 32:19).

I became really excited about that verse. The trouble was that there was no one to share it with. I didn't see another soul until early afternoon, when Mary arrived. Almost before she had got through the door, I bombarded her with my news. And this sort of thing hasn't just happened once. Even now, God keeps on speaking to me clearly and wonderfully through his Word. I'm at last beginning to discover that the Bible is a living book.

It's supposed to be like this!

I must admit I was surprised when I learnt what the Bible could really do in my life. Yet I shouldn't have been surprised—what was happening to me should have been an everyday Christian experience.

I now remember with sadness and shame just how poor my relationship with the Bible had been since my conversion twenty one years ago. Like every good convert I eventually started reading it daily, but this was more of a chore than a joy. I became familiar with the well-known passages and preached regularly in the churches. Yet somehow it didn't come alive.

Nineteen years passed by. No one would have guessed how bad things were. Then gradually I became aware that God was speaking to me through the Scriptures. They started to breathe and live. I began to develop a real appetite for and a new interest in the Bible. I found myself wanting to meditate more deeply and for longer periods of time. I really looked forward to my meeting with God through his Word.

I became dissatisfied with the short portion of Scripture recommended in my daily notes, and often read much more than was required. It was like a voyage of discovery. Passages which I knew very well had new depth and meaning to them. I didn't reject the traditional interpreta-

tions of the various passages, yet for the first time in my life
I was really letting God himself speak to me.

Are you puzzled by such expressions as 'new meaning'
and 'voyage of discovery?' Perhaps you feel that words like
these are far too strong to be genuine. I used to think so too.
Now I find that such descriptions are not at all far-fetched.
They should represent a 'normal' experience in the life of
every Christian.

There is no need for any of us to drag ourselves wearily
through a meaningless daily reading, year after year. God
wants our time with the Bible to be a moving encounter
with himself. However, there are many things we must do
to make this a reality. Two things in particular come to
mind:

First, we need to know what the Bible is, and what it's
supposed to do for us when we read it. Second, we must ask
God to change our dull relationship with the Bible, and to
give us a new and thrilling understanding of it. This is not
the kind of request which we should make lightly. God will
answer us only on his terms. Are you willing, for example,
to clear away the barriers which are preventing him from
changing things?

What is so Special about the Bible?

It's God's Word and he speaks through it

Suppose you were sitting at home reading your Bible and
Jesus walked into the room. Suppose he took away your
Bible and began speaking to you using the actual words of
the passage you had just been reading. How do you think
you'd react? I think you'd listen eagerly. Why? Because
you'd actually be *seeing* Jesus speaking to you!

We tend to see our Bible as being just a book. But it's not.
What you read in it is God's Word. It's God's voice to you
and to me. We listen happily to human speech. How much
more should we be aware of the words of God in the Word
of God!

It helped me to believe when I was converted

Do you remember when God first spoke to you? It's more than likely that at some stage the Bible was used to help you understand the gospel message. As you heard or read some of its contents you became aware that God was speaking through the various verses. As a result, faith sprang up and you believed what you read, and accepted Christ into your life.

What happened was really quite simple. Your faith arose when you allowed the Word of God to affect you. Or as Paul puts it, 'Faith comes from hearing the message, and the message is heard through the word of Christ' (Romans 10:17).

While all this was going on, an amazing thing happened—you were born again. Jesus says that there is a direct link between the new birth and the Bible. 'Born of water (i.e. the Word) and the Spirit' (John 3:5). Peter put it very powerfully: '...born again...through the living and enduring word of God... And this is the word that was preached to you' (1 Peter 1:23 ff).

It still builds up my faith

The big mistake we make is to think of this particular work of the Bible as little more than a past event. But it goes on working, today, tomorrow and for the rest of our lives—if we'll let it. For if faith is to be active it needs to be strengthened through God's Word.

It helps me to grow

God wants me to grow so that I may worship and serve him more effectively. Peter, feeling perhaps that his readers hadn't quite seen the connection between the Bible and their growth, writes,'Crave pure spiritual milk, so that by it you may grow up' (1 Peter 2:2).

A growing Christian is one who is continually learning about God. Although that learning process will be completed in heaven, it begins here on earth, so it's important for us to make a start. Many of us are physically fat and spiritually skinny, so let's reduce our intake of stodge and start to fill ourselves with prime meat, the meat of the Word.

Paul says that the purpose of the Bible is to help us to be 'thoroughly equipped' or 'complete' (2 Timothy 3:17). There is no area of our lives which should remain untouched by God's Word. The whole of me must move towards that completeness, and I need to allow God to do this in his way and time. All he demands is my willingness. The variety of ways in which the Bible helps us to grow is endless, because it's 'living' and 'enduring' (1 Peter 1:23).

It studies me as I study it

Its good for people to study the Bible and to gain a real understanding of it. Many Christians are able to quote chapter and verse on almost any subject. That's very commendable, but God doesn't want head-knowledge alone. He wants changed lives. And that only happens when we let the Word study us. 'The Word of God is living and active... it penetrates even to dividing soul and spirit, joints and marrow; it judges the thoughts and attitudes of the heart' (Hebrews 4:12).

We don't like this idea, do we? It's far safer to pour our energies into looking at God than it is to examine ourselves in the light of what he might be trying to say. 'After all, he might convict me of sin in my life and I wouldn't want that to happen!'

It helps me to survive

We live in a cruel and hostile world. Satan is doing all he can to smash us to pieces. In Paul's day a man without a weapon in the middle of a battle didn't last very long. Nor will the Christian survive in the battle against 'spiritual forces of evil' (Ephesians 6:12) unless he learns to love and use his Bible, which is the sword of the Spirit (Ephesians 6:17). The Bible is more than ink on paper, for when used correctly it carries with it the mighty power of God's Holy Spirit.

You may laugh at the seriousness with which I write

about this warfare. I would have done the same a year or two ago. But not now. The reason I saw no battle is that I was a defeated Christian and my sword lay almost unused.

Since God has moved in my life in a new way, I've discovered what it means to grasp my sword and to use it against the enemy. I wonder how many Christians today are defeated before they set foot on the battlefield because the Word of truth has rusted into its scabbard?

It shows me the way ahead

I'm sorry for those who don't belong to God's family. Without Christ to guide them, they're wandering aimlessly through a dark and frightening maze. They do not know where they're going or even why they exist at all.

Our world is different—it's full of certainty and light because we have Christ, prayer and the Bible to show us who we are and where we're going. We don't need to fall or stumble because 'Your word is a lamp to my feet and a light for my path' (Psalm 119:105).

What Does God Expect to Happen when we Read His Word?

As you'll soon discover, I love gardening. Although I enjoy cultivating flowers, I revel in vegetables most of all. I grow almost all the greens we need throughout the year, plus one or two root crops like beetroot and parsnip.

I prepare the ground well. I'm an organic grower, so I dig in plenty of compost. I sow the seeds on the correct date and every day after breakfast I wander outside in my slippers to see if anything is sprouting. As time goes by I expect to see sturdy young plants developing until finally there's a delicious crop ready to be eaten.

God's Word is like seed, and when he sows it in our lives he expects it to sprout, mature and fruit. That's what the parable of the sower is all about. Unfortunately our spiritual growth is stunted if we miss the point of the parable. We are so used to hearing it applied to the preaching of the gospel to the unbeliever, that we fail to apply it to ourselves. How we love to evade God's voice!

His seed is supposed to germinate not only in the heart of the unbeliever to bring him to faith; it is meant to take root in my life too and it brings me to a deeper faith. It's not just for 'those unbelievers', it's for *me*!

May I suggest that you re-read the parable, but from a different angle. Instead of seeing it as 'this is for non-Christians' story, see it as a 'this is for me' part of the Bible. You'll find that the principles which you used to apply only to gospel preaching apply equally well to you as a Christian. In other words, change your thinking from, 'Non-Christians ought to listen to God's Word' to 'I must hear God's voice through his Word'.

God expects me to listen and obey (i.e. bear fruit)

The number of ways in which God speaks through his Word is truly amazing. He does it through daily readings, sermons, Christian magazines, prayer and conversations. Each time he talks to us he leaves us with a deliberate choice—whether to allow his Word to do what it should in our lives, or to turn a deaf ear to it.

Let me ask you a question. Are you really sure that the Bible is God's Word to you? That may sound a silly question because I'm sure you know the "correct" answer. But what is important is to feel it in your heart as well as knowing it in your head.

St. Paul was thrilled when he found how positive the Thessalonians were concerning God's Word. 'When you received the word of God, which you heard from us, you accepted it not as the word of men, but as it actually is, the word of God, which is at work in you who believe' (1 Thessalonians 2:13).

Let's return to the illustration used earlier of Jesus taking your Bible away and himself speaking the Word to you. In a way the Thessalonians were accepting in their hearts that although the words were Paul's, they were really God's. Because they had the right attitude, God in turn was able to

work in their lives through the Word which he brought via
Paul.

Asking God to Change Things

There was a time when God never really got through to me.
I believed that the Bible was his Word but I came to the
conclusion that it never really spoke to me as it did to others. I
wanted God to say things to me, I wanted a new relationship
with the Scriptures and I prayed about it. He gave me what I
wanted but he expected me to do my share of the work too.
Have you the same problem that I had?

One of the unpleasant jobs I have to do in my garden is to
clear away the weeds. I hate it! I want my crops the easy way.
I often find tender and precious plants being choked to death
by dozens of weeds which are robbing them of light, warmth,
air and moisture. It's a heart-breaking job to untangle the
mess, only to find a spindly pale plant which has been almost
destroyed by those weeds. Jesus said, 'Other seed fell among
thorns, which grew up and choked the plants, so that they did
not bear grain' (Mark 4:7). 'Choked...so they did not bear
grain'—a true picture of many of us today. Choked by 'the
worries of this life, the deceitfulness of riches, and the desires
for other things' (v.19). Some of us are not reading the Bible
at all. Others are reading it but it has little effect—it cannot
grow because it's crowded out.

A Christian like this is lonely. God's voice is muffled and so
he seems remote and unreal. This kind of Christian does not
enjoy rich fellowship because he really has very little to share
with his brothers and sisters in the church. He's isolated,
strangled by the weeds, barely keeping his faith. He's
unhappy but he doesn't know why. The Word cannot grow
because it is choked by boredom, apathy, deadness,
indiscipline, a low expectancy of the power of God's Word
and many other things.

Uproot the Weeds

God will fulfil our desire for a new start but *in his own way*.
First of all I must admit that I need that new start. Asking

God to work in me is something else I can do. But am I willing to pay the price of clearing away the weeds? Removing some of them will be painful and slow and I may often feel that I'm fighting a losing battle. Am I willing to keep on 'pulling up weeds' until the ground is ready for God to do great things in me?

God is ready. He wants to open my eyes anew and to give me a powerful motivation to study his Word. He wants to revolutionise the boredom of my quiet times into an exciting encounter with himself. He wants to change my attitude in church services, and to thrill me with the knowledge that he actually wants to talk with me. And where, I wonder, does he want me to go from here?

Points to Ponder

1. When you hear a sermon, you may do one or more of the following. Which of them is the most frequent response? Which is the least frequent?
   (a) Wait for the speaker to say something interesting?
   (b) Listen for God to speak to you?
   (c) Assess the speaker and his personality?
   (d) Decide how good his sermon is?

2. When you pick up your Bible and read it privately, do you expect God to speak to you then? (often/sometimes/rarely/never)

3. How would you reply to the question Derek asked on page 13: 'What does the Bible mean to you?'

4. How much time do you spend reading or meditating on the Scriptures each day? (0 minutes/up to 5 minutes/5–10 minutes/10–20 minutes/20–30 minutes/ longer than 30 minutes)

5. Do you find it helpful to share with others what God has said to you and to them through the Bible? When does this happen? How often?

6. Do you think that you are "growing" as a result of reading the Word of God?

7. When God challenges you about some area in your life, do you resist his voice or listen to him and act on what he is saying?

8. Can you pick out any reasons in your own life why God's Word might not be affecting you?

"...I USED TO HIDE IN A WARDROBE TO AVOID
BEING TAKEN TO THE PRAYER MEETING..."

3

The Bible Begins to Live
Derek

When my son David was four years old, he wanted to help me with the weeding. Reluctantly, I let him! Although he enjoyed himself, the result was a disaster. Most of my delicate young plants ended up on the compost heap, and the ugly weeds were left standing triumphantly in the flower borders. I couldn't be angry with him—he simply didn't know the difference!

Even a grown-up can make the same mistakes if he's a beginner. Some weeds are so pretty they look like cultivated plants. Others start out so small that it hardly seems worth while pulling them out. Sometimes things are in such a horrible tangle that you don't know where to begin. Some pull out very easily, others are so deep-rooted that when they do come out you fall over backwards.

We face the same kind of problem in our Christian lives. We have to learn to discover which weeds are choking the Word of God. To help us do this, I've described five of the commonest varieties. You probably don't have problems with all of them, but you may have trouble with some which are not listed. So there's no need to feel smug if you find that only one of two of the following need uprooting!

Hardly reading the Bible at all

When I first committed my life to Christ, no one told me I should read the Bible regularly. A year later I had hardly read any of God's book, and I was beginning to backslide.

Things became so bad that I used to hide in a wardrobe to avoid being taken to the prayer meeting each week. (A friend called Andrew used to search for me so that he could escort me to the chapel).

Occasionally I heard other students make comments like, 'John isn't ready yet, he's still having his Q.T.' 'What is this mysterious Q.T.?' I used to wonder. I didn't dare ask anyone in case I looked silly. Was it something like brushing your teeth or sitting on the lavatory? Had my upbringing in the Lancashire Pennines made me ignorant of some important practice? Then, by accident, I discovered that "Q.T." meant a "Quiet Time", although I knew very little about what this might involve.

As a Christian, I didn't grow much in those early years because I wasn't into serious Bible study and meditation. I was undisciplined in my reading even if I did get down to it every day and I rarely spent more than a few minutes scanning the verses. On other occasions, weeks would go by without my so much as glancing at the Scriptures. It's no wonder I didn't grow.

Today I'm saddened by the number of believers who neglect their Bibles as I used to. How can we really expect God to speak to us when we deliberately close his main line of communication? I don't know how many Christians are cultivating this nasty 'weed', but the number is shamefully high.

Where do you stand?

Not expecting anything to happen when I read it

My daughter Sarah goes to birthday parties saying, 'I don't expect I'll win any of the games.' She's often right, and returns home with just the usual balloon and sticky birthday cake in her hand. If she thought she had a chance of winning I feel sure she'd try harder, and would probably do quite well.

My son David and I build electronic flashers and bleepers. I never really expect them to work and because of this I'm rather careless in how I construct them.

There are lots of people who never expect to get anything

out of life. So they don't! They just survive the same boring routine each day. Life is just plain dull.

I can have the same kind of attitude towards reading the Bible. I may be opening its pages day after day without expecting anything interesting or exciting to happen. Maybe my past experience of Bible reading has been rather dull, so I assume it will always be that way. Possibly none of my friends really enjoy reading the Bible, so there is nothing in my conversation with them to whet my appetite.

What Sarah needs is a new attitude towards winning party games. What I need is greater confidence in my ability to build bleepers. What each of us needs is a real sense of expectancy, that next time we read our Bibles we can look to God for something great.

Turning a deaf ear

'Turning a deaf ear'—it's an expression we often hear, because people do it to each other all the time. I do it to Nancy and she does it to me. The next day I can even deny that she told me something or other because I decided not to listen at the time.

This is not just a 'weed' blown in by the wind. It's one which Satan persuades us to plant and carefully cultivate until it takes over our Christian lives. It's an attractive weed because it takes away the pain of being challenged by the Bible. It gets rid of the agony of carrying out some of God's unwelcome commands. Our enemy doesn't want the Word to divide 'soul and spirit, joints and marrow' (Hebrews 4:12). Nor does he want us to allow God to judge 'the thoughts and attitudes of the heart' (Hebrews 4:12). By encouraging us to turn a deaf ear to God, he can stop us from being changed by him.

The Bible is full of stories about the tragedy of those who wouldn't listen, and the triumph of those who would. When the Word of God to the nation was brought through Jeremiah, King Jehoiakim cut up the scroll into small pieces and threw them into the fire (Jeremiah 36:20–26). If only he had paid attention! In New Testament times, the religious leaders couldn't hear what Stephen was saying so they 'covered their ears and…all rushed at him' (Acts 7:57).

Some did listen to God. Paul was one of them. His life was totally changed when he heard and obeyed God's commands while he was on the Damascus road. Apart from individuals, there were whole congregations who took God's word seriously, and the results were tremendous. 'When you received the word of God…you accepted it not as the word of men but as it actually is, the word of God' (1 Thessalonians 2:13).

Jesus ended the parable of the sower by saying, 'He who has ears to hear, let him hear' (Mark 4:9). He then went on to explain that those who decided not to listen to God, become steadily more deaf to his voice. On the other hand, those who do listen are given the privilege of hearing more and more wonderful things.

There seems to be no comfortable middle position—each of us is either hardening towards God or becoming more open to him. Which is it to be in my life and yours? Jesus wants to open our ears so that we may know a greater closeness to him and deeper joy in our lives—'Blessed are…your ears because they hear' (Matthew 13:16). He asks me to be honest about my attitude to his Word and to seek his help if this weed is in my life.

While I was writing this chapter I discovered that my left ear had gone deaf. It must have slowly become clogged with wax, but I hadn't noticed. I did the sensible thing and asked the doctor to syringe it. As I walked out of the surgery my ear recognised a whole range of sounds which had been previously blocked by the wax. Maybe God needs to do this with my spiritual ears.

It's just a book for discussing

The early Church was often troubled by false teachers. They entertained the Christians by arguing with each other in public, using the Bible as a basis for their meaningless discussions. There were other 'teachers' too, who could talk for hours on the subject of the genealogies of Scripture. They never actually achieved anything, but it really didn't matter, so long as they were well paid and the people admired them.

'I don't treat the Bible like that!' you may protest. 'I read and study it seriously'. May I ask you to apply one or two acid tests to your attitude towards Scripture!

Do you find yourself saying (either in private or in group Bible study) 'Isn't it interesting that...?' Are you highly critical or over-fussy about those whose interpretation of the Bible is slightly different from yours? Do you crusade against Bible versions you don't like? Are you a hairsplitter when you discuss Christianity?

If your answers are 'yes', then you are probably too detached from the Bible. You could be treating the study of it (and your Christianity) as an intellectual exercise, rather than a life-changing encounter with the living Word.

My relationship with the Bible (and with God) used to be like that—correct but very cold. I used to examine the Word but I never let it examine me. The Holy Spirit had to open my eyes to the purpose and richness of the Scriptures. As he did so, the Bible and I became deeply attached friends. My daily readings became times of real involvement, even to the point of sometimes bringing tears to my eyes.

How involved are you with your Bible?

I'm just doing my Christian duty

Some Christians genuinely believe that they have a good relationship with the Bible simply because they go through the routine of reading a portion of it each day. Often it's done mechanically, as a kind of duty to God and to keep their consciences clear. They do it because they ought to, not because they really want to. It's rather like my children's attitude to washing their faces—they do it only because I expect them to, not because they see any real value in it.

It's true that God wants us to read the Bible and we should encourage one another to do this. But we miss the whole point of the exercise if we plough through a lot of verses each morning and never get anything out of them.

The Bible is meant to speak to us—as a group gathered on Sunday mornings, yes, but more especially to me as an individual. It should be my personal handbook to life.

I shouldn't be approaching the Word of God out of a sense of duty but out of the desire to know what God wants to tell me. Something should happen to me as I read it. I should be challenged, uplifted, warned, informed, guided or instructed by it. As I read, I should be asking myself, 'Now what is God trying to say to me from this?' When my attitude is positive, God can and will open the Scriptures to me. He may not speak as much through some passages as he does through others, but he'll still speak.

If 'It's my duty' is your weed, why not ask God to help you pull it up by changing your attitude to Bible-reading? It may be hard-going at first but God can make what now seems to be a duty into a real desire.

Let the Bible get to Work on Us

Once we recognise weeds and begin pulling them up, there's room for us to grow. The Bible is free to perform all kinds of valuable tasks in our lives. It will comfort, teach, challenge and guide us. Our faith will be sustained and built up. We shall be better equipped to survive in a godless world.

We have to develop a really close relationship with our Bibles. Paul says, '*Let* the word of Christ *dwell* in you richly' (Colossians 3:16). The word 'dwell' means to be at home. That's the kind of friendship we need—where the Word is completely free to settle down comfortably in every part of our lives. That relationship can become so deep and natural that it affects us constantly as the living, active, abiding Word spreads into our lives and experiences.

It's our decision to *let* this friendship develop. God won't force it. How can this happen to us? It will happen if we simply allow God to speak as we meditate upon his Word.

The amount of time we spend with our Bibles is important. So is the quality of that daily meeting together. Most of us tend to rush things. We treat our Bible reading in the same way as brushing our teeth before going out. We leap (or roll wearily!) out of bed, hurry through the reading set for the day (hoping it won't be a long one this time), whizz through the prayer list and dash off to the next urgent activity. That's it, done! But is that really the best way to enjoy a valuable relationship? Would we do that when we were meeting our best friend? Of course not!

The word 'meditation' may arouse suspicion in some readers. True, the non-Christian cults use the expression, but so does the Bible! It's the opposite of rushing. It means reading a passage of Scripture, then slowly pondering over the whole portion, or just a single verse which seems especially important. It should be done in an attitude of prayer so that God can quietly talk to us. Often it's good to clear away all previous ideas about a passage, so that God can speak freely, perhaps in a fresh way.

If your time of study and prayer has been neglected, you won't find success overnight. It will be something of an uphill struggle at first and there will be a strong temptation to give up. It will take time, effort and patience to develop the habit of meditation. You may feel you can manage only a few minutes with a very small number of verses. It may not be a good idea to read too long a passage, or to tackle difficult parts of the Bible, because it can be discouraging.

Being open-minded

It's amazing how we can deceive ourselves into thinking we are open-minded, when in fact our minds are totally closed. That's how I was and I didn't know it. The change in me has been tremendous. It's like having a new pair of eyes. I've had a good knowledge of the Bible for many years yet it now seems as though I hardly know anything at all. I'm learning all over again.

Ten years ago I thought I understood the meaning of most parts of the Bible. I knew where I stood on all the major doctrines and practices. I was completely closed to any other way of seeing things. I was like a programmed computer. If I listened to a sermon or conversation which differed from my interpretation of Scripture I automatically rejected it. I was critical and hostile towards people who dared to disagree with my viewpoint because they were 'wrong'.

Things were easy most of the time in my narrow little world because I carefully avoided Christians who were different. But God put me into a position where I was forced to rub shoulders with those I used to accuse of being 'unscriptural'. They had a real love for the Bible which I hadn't. The Lord was so real to them that I envied that closeness. Some of their doctrines were slightly different from mine and yet they were open-minded. They were willing to discuss my views and to accept me as I was.

God used these warm-hearted people to melt my hard heart. I became more willing to take a new look at the minor points of doctrine on which I'd been so stubborn. I certainly haven't rejected most of my past teaching but I am willing to re-examine some of my former interpretations.

One of the areas of greatest re-thinking was the question of Christian experiences. I had always opposed the idea that the emotions were involved in Christianity. My brand of Christianity was cold and intellectual. My relationships reflected my theology which said that a mature Christian must be detached and isolated from other Christians.

Verses like, 'God has poured out his love into our hearts' (Romans 5:5) were just truths to be accepted with the mind. They were not meant to be 'felt'. I was completely mistaken. As soon as I knew that I could experience God's love, a new warmth developed in my relationship with him. I also discovered that the filling of the Spirit in Ephesians 5:18 is meant to be felt, otherwise why would Paul have contrasted it with drunkenness? I've never been drunk, but from what I've seen it's not just something you think about—it's an experience!

I used to persecute those who believed that New Testament miracles could happen today. I'd decided that they disappeared at the end of the apostolic age, and so that was that! Once again my interpretation was wrong, and I'm now beginning to see the power of God at work in my own life and ministry.

Dare we risk opening our hearts and minds to the extent that we have to re-think some of our interpretations? It could mean more than just a change of opinion—it may turn our Christian lives upside down!

What about God?

Most of what's been written so far has been concerned with the steps *we* must take. *We* must clear the weeds, *we* must allow the Bible to do its job, and *we* must meditate on it with an open mind. So where does God come into it?

Without the work of God in our lives, all these efforts will fail. We will remain only partially-sighted like the man in Mark 8:24 who saw people as though they were trees walking around. What he needed was a second touch from Jesus to help him to see properly. It's the same in our relationship with the Bible. We may need to ask God for another touch of his power to open our eyes still further. We can't open our own eyes to the greatness of the Bible, nor work up a bigger appetite for reading it. Only he can do that.

The Lord commands us to ask, seek and knock for the good things he wants to provide for us (Matthew 7:17). One of the good things must surely be the enjoyment of his Word. So we can ask God with complete confidence that he will say 'yes' to our request for that new relationship with the Bible.

We may wonder whether this will happen overnight. Sometimes it does, but not always. Our decision to seek more of his Word may be an instant one, but the answer will be in God's time. For some, it will be a gradual process. For others, nothing will happen for quite a while, then suddenly everything will change.

We may wonder what it will be like. It certainly won't be dull! By way of illustration let's recall what happened in Nehemiah's day when the people re-discovered the Law. They were so excited that they listened to it being read for six hours. There was no sign of boredom—'All the people listened attentively' (Nehemiah 8:3). God was working so powerfully in their lives that they couldn't wait to hear what

he had to say to them from the Law. They were simply
overflowing with joy—'All the people lifted their hands
and responded, "Amen! Amen!" Then they bowed down
and worshipped the Lord with their faces to the ground'
(v.6).

Praise and worship were not the only things that happened. Over the next few weeks they studied the Law and
discovered some practices which had been neglected for
years. Because the Law now meant something to them, they
immediately began to obey God's written commands. In
addition to arranging a seven-day festival, they fasted,
cleansed their relationships and confessed their sins. In
other words, their lives were turned upside down when they
responded to God's Word.

Similar things are happening today in the lives of
individuals and churches. Thousands of God's people are
re-discovering the hidden treasures in their Bibles. There's
a new thirst for Bible study and private meditation. What
used to be dry and dusty pages are now crammed full of
powerful and relevant teaching. The Bible's not changing of
course—it's the readers who are!

To put it in a nutshell, a genuine openness to the Bible
opens up a whole new world—the world of New Testament
Christianity. As a result, people are eagerly searching out
what it really means to be a joyful and fulfilled Christian.
God becomes much closer when we find out what he's
actually like by reading the Bible. Relationships with other
Christians become deeper. At last we've got something
worth sharing with each other. Instead of gossiping about
this and that, we talk together about what God has taught us
today from his Word. And that's worth telling everyone
about!

Points to Ponder

1. Look at this list of "weeds". Which, if any, are you cultivating in your Christian life?
   (a) Hardly reading the Bible at all.
   (b) Not expecting anything to happen when I read it.
   (c) Turning a deaf ear.
   (d) Seeing it as a "book for discussing".
   (e) Reading it simply as a "Christian duty".
   Are there other "weeds"? What can you do about them?

2. Do you meditate on Scripture? If you do, is this a valuable experience for you?

3. When you come across an interpretation of Scripture different from your own, do you reject it at once? Why does this happen? Are you ready to re-think your viewpoint? Could this be dangerous?

4. 'Thousands of God's people are rediscovering the hidden treasures in their Bibles' (p. 34). What advice would you give to somebody who wanted to become one of these?

" I SWEPT MY RUBBER PLANT UP IN MY ARMS
AND DANCED IT ROUND THE ROOM..."

4

Worship Him
Mary

Built into every human being is the need to worship something. The unbeliever finds his god in a relationship, a career, a home, an ambition or in some material possession. He spends time with it, talks about it and discovers some measure of fulfilment in life because of it. If it's removed or broken, he searches for a new god and worships that instead.

The Christian knows that God should be the prime object of his worship because the Bible makes that quite clear. 'You shall have no other gods before me' (Exodus 20:3). He realises that God deserves and desires to be worshipped not only because of what he's done but because of who he is. 'Worship the Lord in the splendour of his holiness' (1 Chronicles 16:29). It scarcely needs to be said that the child of God has an advantage over the man of the world because he knows the Person who will never desert him (Hebrews 13:5) and he's found the One he was made to rejoice in (Isaiah 43:21). His worship has the potential of being the most satisfying of all.

What sort of worship is satisfying?

The trouble is that different individuals have different ideas of what sort of worship is satisfying. I remember one lively meeting I attended in a small church building. The service began with quiet, worshipful choruses and I was more than happy to join in. However, as time went on, the noise increased and I started to feel very uncomfortable. Before long, I was completely overwhelmed by the crescendo of sound from organ, guitars, drums and tambourines. Whispered words of adoration increased in volume and then, in their enthusiasm, nearly everyone burst out in tongues. The whole scene was one of great confusion. I stood there for a while, not knowing whether or not to be involved and almost unable to think straight. Was this true worship? Finally, still surrounded by noise and chaos, I prayed, 'Can you hear me, Lord?' I'm still wondering if he could!

On the other hand, I've been to more formal services where everything has been worked out to fit into a certain period of time. The people simply follow the order of events, singing, praying or listening when they should and generally accepting all that's happening. Their faces often reveal no sign of excitement or adoration of God at all. Is this form of worship satisfying? A happy heart is supposed to make the face cheerful (Proverbs 15:13). However, I almost gain the impression that it doesn't matter how miserable you look or how you're feeling. It seems that 'the service' is, in itself, regarded as 'worship'. If you attend it and join in, you've automatically been 'worshipping'.

We can so easily race into worship without thinking. We can beat our tambourines and appear to be expressing worship without any heart-involvement at all. The mask words, 'Glory!' and 'Hallelujah!' may deceive those around us but not God. Similarly, we can go to our orderly 'worship' services and be so immersed in correctness that we never do actually 'worship' the Lord.

Talking to the woman of Samaria, Jesus tells us that God seeks worshippers whose hearts are involved in worship. 'The true worshippers will worship the Father in spirit and truth, for they are the kind of worshippers the Father seeks' (John 4:23).

People in New Testament times who really worshipped Jesus weren't forced to do so, they wanted to. God would rather have worshippers who wanted to worship him than those who did so out of duty alone. Those only feeling an obligation to worship are often limited to an outward show of affection which is generally very superficial. On the human level, when a young man falls in love with a girl, he worships her. He thinks about her almost constantly, he buys things to please her and he goes out of his way to meet her 'accidentally'! The girl hasn't said to him, 'You must worship me'. He wants to praise her because he loves her.

Only when our motivation to praise God emerges out of love for him will we be able to worship in spirit and truth. When we've examined our motivation, we'll realise whether or not our actions are really coming from an inner sense of adoration. This is the only sort of worship that can be truly satisfying.

Worship is emotional

Worship is a matter of the heart. It's an expression of love to God, and love isn't cold and hard, it's emotional. It's true that noisy, unrestrained worship should be viewed with suspicion, but worship which involves the expression of genuine feelings of adoration should be welcomed. Jesus himself effectively encouraged it. When he rode into Jerusalem, the crowds around him flung their clothes on the road and cut branches from the trees for him to walk on. They shouted and cheered as he entered the city. The religious leaders couldn't stand such unorthodox behaviour and tried to make Jesus silence his worshippers but he refused (Matthew 21:8–16; Luke 19:35–40).

Emotion in worship isn't always expressed in such a lively and enthusiastic way. On one occasion, Jesus was having dinner at the house of Simon, the Pharisee. A sinful woman came in and knelt down behind the Lord. She wept over his feet, kissed them, wiped them with her hair and poured perfume on them (Luke 7:36–50). Her worship was definitely emotional, but it was a different sort of worship from that of the crowds who later welcomed Jesus into Jerusalem. Jesus gladly received the loud praises of the jubilant people and also the silent adoration of the woman.

Worship is extravagant

If love is at the heart of worship, then we should expect worship to be extravagant and even sacrificial. The more a boy and girl love one another, the more they'll do for each other. They'll share money, possessions and time, not so much because they've got to, but because they want to. When Mary anointed Jesus she was condemned for being reckless in her actions. The disciples thought that the ointment should have been sold and the money given to the poor. It should have been used in service, not in worship. The woman's generosity was too great—maybe even too challenging for them. But all she was doing was proving her love for Jesus by what she was willing to give him (John 12:1–8). Jesus loved us so much that he was willing to die a cruel death on the cross for us. How great our love for him should be! How extravagant is our worship in terms of money, possessions, time—indeed, of our whole lives?

Individual Worship

Unless we as individuals are gaining experience in private worship, we can hardly expect great times of praise to come when we meet with other Christians. Perhaps daily individual worship isn't something we've ever thought too seriously about. If we do spend time with God, we tend to pray for things rather than praise. Maybe we feel that time spent in worship is time wasted. We'd rather tell God what we want than how we feel about him.

Books or sermons on worship may challenge us to review our ways, but what usually happens is that for two days we make a frantic attempt at praise and then return to normal! We can worship God when we feel like it but when we don't, we quickly give up on the idea. 'Maybe it's only meant to be done with others after all,' we think and confine the activity to when we meet with them.

Although the Bible sees worship mainly as a shared experience, there are also times when individuals glorified Jesus. The woman who anointed his feet is a good example of this, but there are also other people who fell before him and expressed their praise. God is seeking worshippers. He's looking for individuals who are keen to learn the secret and joy of how to praise him effectively. He never forces us to worship him, but he invites each one of us to move on into a deeper experience of his presence and power as we lift our hearts to him in love.

The wise man built his house upon the rock

Everyone want instant worship! We all want to come to God and immediately feel that we're 'in the heavenlies' with him! This does happen on occasions, but not often. Why not? The reason is that we try to build our 'worship houses' on sand. Worship has become something we do quickly and easily. It's 'bashing a tambourine' or 'singing a well-known hymn'! Our experience of worship can be just as shallow as that of the unbeliever when he's acting or singing at a Christmas carol service.

God seeks worshippers who'll build their worship houses on rock. He wants them to count the cost. Are they willing to pay for the materials they need, or will their resources only last up to the third row of bricks? In other words, how keen are they about worshipping him? Do they plan to spend time and effort digging the foundations in their lives, or would they rather treat their worship as a sort of hobby? A lazy builder will work fast and use poor materials. Even if he believes that his worship is stable, the strong winds of calamity will beat against it, and it will collapse and be silenced. But the individual who realises that his worship cannot be built in a day will persevere through all hardships. 'Bad weather' or 'delays in the best supplies' won't deter him at all. He'll live to experience a deep, satisfying worship which will enable him to stand against every disaster that comes to him.

Obstacles

A sinful heart

If a boy and girl have an argument, or if one of them has done something to hurt the other, then they're hardly likely to be in the mood to praise each other. In public they may give the impression that everything's fine. They may hold hands or talk as if nothing were wrong. Yet underneath there are bitter feelings and unhealed wounds which only they know anything about.

If worship comes from our hearts, it's pointless for us to attempt to worship God when our hearts are full of evil. Time and time again the Scriptures reveal that it's our sins which hide God's face from us and which cause him not to hear us (Psalm 66:17,18; Isaiah 59:1–3). This is why many of our attempts at praising God seem to get us nowhere.

We are experts at harbouring sin in our lives and calling it by some other name. Thus, a grudge against someone becomes a 'personality clash', the removal of some stationery from work is regarded as a 'perk' and a piece of juicy gossip is considered an 'item for urgent prayer'. We must learn how to recognise sin for what it is. A well-known store has recently tried to do this by changing the signs on its doors. Whereas they once read, 'Shoplifters will be prosecuted', they now warn, 'Thieves will be prosecuted'. What's the difference between a shoplifter and a thief? Nothing. 'Shoplifter' is just a more palatable word in today's society than 'thief'. But when we call sin by its real name we can do something about it. Sin requires confession, repentance and healing before we can know any release in worship. If we're not sure whether or not we're harbouring it in our lives, we should be humble enough to seek advice.

An over-active body

Can busyness be sinful? Surely this implication is found in the story of Mary and Martha where Jesus rebukes Martha for her over-activity (Luke 10:38–42). Somehow we seem to find plenty of time to spend serving God. We're happy to be involved in all kinds of Christian activities but frequently fail to choose 'what is better'. We neglect the habit of sitting at Jesus' feet and simply loving him. Often, even though we know that we're excessively active, we do nothing about it. God convicts us for a while, but his Word falls on poor soil and it never actually takes root in our experience.

Even if we do manage to persuade our bodies to stop for God, our minds often remain busy. Worshipping God is fine if we're in the mood but often we're not. This is particularly true when we've just rolled out of bed when our desire to praise is probably non-existent! We may make a few vain attempts, but before two minutes have passed we remember that we've got to do something. We're afraid that we'll forget it if we don't do it now, so we interrupt our worship and on our return, remember a list of other things to sort out. Our thoughts wander round the world or become focused on some important or disastrous event which has happened or may possibly be about to happen. Our worship time ends up by being a few scrambled praise words followed by an assortment of snores and a cup of coffee! 'The spirit is willing, but the body is weak' (Matthew 26:41).

So where are the worshippers whom God seeks? Many of them have begun well, but their enthusiasm has declined when they've realised that 'worship house-building' isn't always easy. When they've encountered difficulties, they've sat down on site, had a prolonged coffee break and never returned to work.

But there are others who've learnt how to persist in worship regardless of all outward circumstances. They've met with the same problems as their friends but they've kept building. They've been prepared to dig out the sins in their lives and to rejoice no matter how they're feeling. They've met with some disastrous times of praise but they've also experienced some glorious moments of deep, fulfilling worship. Through these, they know that God is glorified and that they are blessed.

How do I Worship God?

Scripture gives us no definite rules to follow, only stories about people who worshipped. These are all different because individuals are different and express their praise in different ways. God is a God of variety. He didn't make all the flowers red, nor did he create identical people. He wants each of us to discover how to enjoy worshipping and loving him in our own individual ways. The more adventurous of us will be keen to experiment with new methods whereas others may prefer more traditional forms. Here are a few ideas to work from.

'I will sing and make music' (Psalm 108:1)

Christian tapes or records are highly effective for creating a worshipful atmosphere. This is true not only when they're used just before a regular time of praise and prayer, but also at other times in the day. I'm rarely separated from my tape recorder. I play Scripture songs on it when I drive to and from work and I sometimes listen to Christian music when I'm alone in my flat. Often I become almost lost in the melodies or words. On occasions I get quite excited and join in, clapping my hands to the rhythms and singing joyfully. But during the quieter choruses I'll probably sit or kneel (if I'm at home) and sing or hum softly, allowing the words to penetrate and lift my heart to God.

When I'm not listening to music, I'm frequently playing it on my guitar and singing (the people living above me know all about that!). Instruments really help worship and God loves to hear us use our talents to glorify him—even when we're alone. If we're very adventurous, we could even try putting a psalm or a prayer to music. I've occasionally done this and have been quite surprised at the result. It's taken a great deal of courage for me to look a fool in my own company! However, once I've started playing a few chords on my guitar, I've found it fairly easy to sing direct from God's Word while making up my own tune as I've gone along. I've discovered that singing in tongues can be uplifting too.

'I meditate on all your works' (Psalm 143:5)

When I'm feeling miserable and fed up, I find it very hard to think of things to say to God in praise. Sometimes when this happens I borrow someone else's words and read aloud a hymn or one of the psalms. Then I muse on it and try to allow its praise to sink into me. If I sit for long enough thinking over what I've read, I often break out of my misery into real joy.

Then there are times when I just sit at a window and gaze outside or actually walk out into the garden. I try to look at beautiful things and appreciate their creation, and I'll talk to God as if he were right beside me. When I'm outside I'll wander around touching, smelling or listening and my heart will go out to the Lord for all his wonderful acts. There's so much joy in simple, almost childlike worship.

'David... danced before the Lord with all his might' (2 Samuel 6:14)

Many Christians condemn the use of our bodies in worship. Michael despised King David because of his 'outrageous' behaviour, but he was simply declaring his joy in a physical way. I frequently raise my hands to praise the Lord—in fact I often find that I can't help raising them. They almost have minds of their own and want to be uplifted to their Maker. I once climbed a tree to worship God and sometimes I've felt so involved in some lively music that I've actually danced to it. On one of these occasions, I swept my rubber plant up in my arms and danced it round the room because I felt such joy and couldn't find any other way to express it! The rubber plant died soon afterwards—of shock no doubt!

'Let us bow down in worship, let us kneel' (Psalm 95:6)

God is holy but I've laughed with him and I've wept before him. Sometimes I just can't say or do anything. I simply kneel and worship in silence. He understands and he rejoices to see his children singing, talking, dancing, laughing and crying before him—just as any earthly father would.

Love for others

If I discover how to worship God on my own, I'll naturally be very much more at ease when I'm praising him with others. However, that doesn't mean that what I do in private is automatically acceptable in public, no matter how 'biblical' it may be.

True worship is not only motivated by love for God, it's also controlled by love for others. The person who's looking for adventure and variety as he worships with others must also be sensitive to the opinions and feelings of those around him. His love and concern for them may prevent him from being as free as he might wish to be in his praise. Similarly, the person who's offended by 'new ideas' in worship mustn't criticise those who want to try them out. His love and care for them will allow them to be free to glorify God in their own way. I need to bend to accommodate you just as you need to do the same for me. That can be hard when we don't agree with each other's approach—but the way of love is never easy. Jesus went to the cross to show us that. If I fix my eyes on God and remain open to his instruction, he'll lead me in worship, and he'll do the same for you. Let's follow the way of love and learn how to worship happily together.

The Results of Worship

At the beginning of this chapter I suggested that only the Christian has the potential for experiencing the highest form of worship because only he has found the One he was made to glorify. As we build up a habit of worship, we'll become more at one with him and not only will his name be exalted but something will happen to us too.

We'll discover a deepening awareness of God's greatness and through this, we'll realise that if he's so mighty then all our troubles can safely be left in his hands. The knowledge that God is in control and understands all that happens to us will give us a tremendous sense of stability. As a result, we'll love him more and trust him to put before us only those things which will enable us to grow as Christians. Then we'll find ourselves able to worship him even when things around us are apparently falling apart. James puts it all in a nutshell, 'Consider it pure joy, my brothers, whenever you face trials of many kinds, because you know that the testing of your faith develops perseverance. Perseverance must finish its work so that you may be mature and complete, not lacking anything' (James 1:2–4).

Job put these words into practice. In his time, he was the most righteous man on earth (Job 1:8) yet disaster struck his family and livelihood. His sons, daughters and servants were killed, his oxen were stolen and his sheep were consumed by fire. When told of what had happened, he 'tore his robe and shaved his head. Then he fell to the ground in worship and said: "Naked I came from my mother's womb, and naked I shall depart. The Lord gave and the Lord has taken away; may the name of the Lord be praised"' (1:20,21).

How could this man have worshipped God when his whole life had been ripped apart? Surely we have the answer at the beginning of the chapter. Here, we learn that Job kept his life free from evil and that he made sacrifices to God for his children in case they sinned. We read that 'this was Job's regular custom' (1:5). The foundations of his life had been dug deep long beforehand. He'd prepared for the day of disaster by building up a life of regular praise and dedication to God, so that in time of deepest trial his faith held firm.

Peter and John were stripped, beaten and secured in the stocks of the inner cell of a prison in Philippi. Yet it was their prayers and worship that began the whole chain of events leading to the conversion of the jailer and his entire household. Maybe God's reason for allowing his servants to suffer was so that the jailer and his family could become Christians. How differently the story might have turned out had Peter and John grumbled about and resented their miserable situation.

The casual worshipper will find it hard suddenly to start worshipping God in a crisis, but those who've spent time developing lives of praise will take every disaster in their stride and rejoice (even in tears) through them all. Their confidence in God and air of triumph will completely baffle the unbelievers (and possibly many believers) around them.

In this way, God's name will be glorified and many will be drawn to him.

Can we imagine what sort of impact a church or fellowship of such victorious worshipping Christians could have in a neighbourhood? It's something to think about—and to act on.

Points to Ponder

1. Why do you worship God? Because you 'ought' to or because you 'want' to? Does it matter?

2. In a church service, do you ever ask yourself if you're really worshipping God? Or do you follow the expected pattern without asking this sort of question?

3. Is it possible to worship God without feeling or showing any kind of emotion?

4. Do you find it easier to pray to God than to praise him?

5. How do you react to the idea of 'learning' how to praise?

6. Several obstacles to worship have been mentioned in this chapter. What particular things hinder you from worshipping God?

7. The chapter mentions several different ways of praising God. Which of these do you think are worth trying? Can you think of any others you would like to experiment with?

8. Are you prepared to be criticised for a sincere attempt at worshipping God even when you're trying to be sensitive to the feelings of others?

9. Are you willing to allow other people to worship God as they want to without criticising them?

10. God is still searching for people who will worship him in Spirit and Truth—will he find you?

" I KNEW ONLY A "PRAYER-LIST"
RELATIONSHIP WITH GOD..."

5

Prayer—Dreary and Dull?

Mary

When we go to our church prayer meetings, what do we get out of them? I sometimes wonder what sort of replies I'd get if I went round asking church members that question. Do we really think at all deeply about why we attend? Maybe it's a life-long habit that keeps us going, or the feeling that we ought to be there, or even an interest in the time of Bible study. What's your reason?

It's very easy for believers to drift into a dull routine without even realising it. Familiar prayer meeting patterns can be repeated so many times that they become 'the norm'. When that happens it's hard to break free and allow God to move in new ways.

What kind of meeting?

Some people, although they may say that they're open to God, really don't want him to interfere with their prayer meeting. They are accustomed to a particular procedure and are offended by and fearful of the slightest change in it. 'It's got to be about the same every week,' they declare, and threaten to leave the church unless they have their own way.

Other people want everything altered. They can't stand the rigid style of meeting and long for freedom in the Spirit. 'It's got to be different every week,' they declare and threaten to leave unless it is.

So we end up with two groups of Christians pulling in opposite directions. What usually happens is that the church adopts a safe middle course which tends, more than anything, towards a routine. Those who resist change are satisfied, the majority of those who remain conform and a handful leave the church altogether.

'Each of you should look not only to your own interests, but also to the interests of others. Your attitude should be the same as that of Christ Jesus who…made himself nothing…' (Philippians 2:4-6ff).

The Son of God fixed his eyes on his Father and laid aside everything to please him. Jesus is our example today but still many of us are stubborn and selfish individuals who refuse to have anything but our own way. We close our minds to Jesus' humility and love. We put our desires before his and those of others, and the whole Church suffers as a result.

We've got to learn how to put God's desires first. We need to rediscover what coming together with him can really be like. The prayer meeting will come to life if God is its guide, but only if we work with him and are open to his will.

Sharing ideas

There are some church members who have thought about how their prayer meeting might be improved but who've never felt that they're able to share their ideas. In the past they've kept quiet or have been ignored but they long to be involved in some decision-making if only in a very small way.

For a long time some church leaders' ideas seem to have dominated the prayer meeting. Perhaps they need to let go a bit more often and allow the ordinary church members to give their opinions about it too. Questionnaires are often seen in our streets so why not in our churches? It would certainly help to make the individual feel that his ideas mattered. Surely the prayer meeting ought to be not so much a concern of the minority as the joint responsibility of the entire church.

Giving and receiving

It's not simply a matter of what we get out of our church prayer meeting, but, almost more important, of what we put into it—do we in fact go for what we can receive or because we want to give?

Every Tuesday at college we had a time when the various tutorial groups went off with their tutors for fellowship. In my group I discovered that all would be well if at least one person came along with something to talk about. But what usually happened was that everyone expected everyone else to arrive with a topic to discuss. The result was generally a complete disaster. We'd skip from subject to subject, get thoroughly bored and be glancing at our watches every few minutes to see how much longer we were going to have to endure.

The same thing happens in some church prayer meetings. People attend not to give but to receive. Everybody else is expected to do the sharing and we find many different reasons why we can't join in too.

The Scriptures tell me that I'm a vital part in the body of Christ and that my contribution is valuable (1 Corinthians 12:12–31). If I persist in holding back, the Church suffers because I'm robbing it by not being willing to participate, and I suffer too. I don't get anything out of the prayer meeting because I refuse to put anything into it. Maybe the real reason why I don't join in is simple—I can't. My own prayer life is so stale and dull that I just haven't got anything at all to share with anyone else.

Praying Alone

God can transform my church prayer meeting but he doesn't need only John and Mike and Ruth to do it. He needs me. Before I can expect the Lord to move in a corporate way. I've got to be open to his working in me as an individual. If most of us at a prayer-meeting have a poor relationship with God, our prayers will get us nowhere. But if each of us is truly seeking him we'll bring his power and love into every function we attend. So in my own private prayer life am I really living close to God, or is he a far-away figure whom I rarely ever meet?

How to embarrass a church member

Perhaps one of the most embarrassing questions you could put to many Christians would be: 'What did the Lord teach you in your quiet time this morning?' If we were honest, we might have to admit that our quiet times, if they exist at all, are almost worthless. When we do have them, we either race through them to get them out of the way or we ramble on at great length without saying anything at all.

Derek and I were once like that. Derek was one of those people who enjoyed active Christian service but who never bothered to pray for longer than three minutes each day. To him, prayer was a burden, something he'd rather not bother with. He knew he ought to do it but instead, plunged himself into all sorts of activities and somehow managed to avoid taking prayer too seriously.

I was totally different. Whenever I could, I escaped church activities. Instead, I shut myself away and spent long periods each day in prayer. But my devotions were legalistic and boring. I knew only a 'prayer-list' relationship with God and week after week he heard the same old routine: 'Father please bless Sue and guide her in your way, and bless and encourage John in his work for you and...

I expect you'll be able to identify with one of us. Derek was too busy to give God his personal attention, and I was too isolated from people and prayed vaguely to the Lord. The one thing that we had in common was that although we'd both been Christians for some while, neither of us could say we had a real relationship with our Heavenly Father.

Duty or privilege?

The Bible says lots about prayer. It's encouraged all through the New Testament. The disciples were told to 'pray and not give up' (Luke 18:1), '(be) faithful in prayer' (Romans 12:12), 'keep on praying' (Ephesians 6:18), 'devote yourselves to prayer' (Colossians 4:2), 'pray continually' (1 Thessalonians 5:17). Many of us know that we should pray but see prayer as a duty and not something to be enjoyed. 'You don't get enthusiastic about it,' we declare, 'you just do it'.

So we approach our prayer-times with the attitude: 'O well, I suppose I'd better pray' and as a result we are bored within the first five minutes. What we're actually doing is to assume that prayer is and always will be a dull duty. But do we honestly believe that God wants us to be thoroughly bored in his company? Is he really such a dreary person to be with and to talk to?

Being with Jesus

How did people react to Jesus when he was on earth? The vivid gospel of Mark tells us the people 'came to him from everywhere' (1:45), 'a crowd gathered so that he and his disciples were not even able to eat' (3:20), 'the crowd that gathered around him was so large that he got into a boat' (4:1), 'A large crowd followed and pressed around him' (5:24). There are many other references as well.

Did these people follow Jesus out of duty? Of course not! They flocked to him because they wanted to be with him. You couldn't have kept them away.

That New Testament Jesus is the same person today as he was then. But we Christians simply can't believe that when we pray we're actually talking to the same Jesus as the Bible people knew. We don't get excited when we meet him in our quiet times (assuming that we have them), and we always want proof that he's there—we want to feel good, we want to see him. But because he's invisible we don't think he meets us when we pray so we don't bother at all, or we almost tape record our devotions and reel them off like parrots.

Our minds tell us that Jesus is there when we pray but our hearts say that we're talking to the ceiling and that only the odd word ever reaches heaven. We've lost, or have never really known what it's like to spend time with the New Testament Jesus who, by his radiant personality, drew crowds to himself.

Derek's great mistake was that he expected prayer to be dull and uninteresting. He plodded along quite happily in his Christian life and was satisfied when he'd done his three minutes a day routine. He never questioned whether God heard his voice or not and the experiences of others gave him the idea that prayer could never be anything more than just a necessary duty.

My great mistake lay in that I focused my attention on prayer and not on Jesus. I had a superb relationship with my prayer list, but not with the living God beyond it. I cultivated a ritual, not a relationship. My quiet times bored me because I never invited Jesus to join me in them.

Then God began to work in us. He showed us that Jesus didn't come to earth to force us to pray, but to give us a real relationship with himself. He was as dissatisfied with our poor attitudes and rituals as we were. 'It needn't be like that,' he seemed to say. 'Invite me back into your quiet times, expect me to change them, and you'll find you'll enjoy my company.' And he was right.

Christians often tell themselves that they've got to get down to more serious prayer. They work hard at it for a few days and then give up. I've done this sort of thing too. I've been convicted about some area in my life and for a while I've battled to put it right. Then after a week or so I'm back where I started. 'What's gone wrong?' I've thought. 'Why do I find it so hard to change?'

I think I've discovered what I was doing wrong. I was listening to the voice which tried to compel me to change and I was struggling to obey it. But in Romans 12:2 we read, 'Be transformed', not, 'Transform yourself.' I was striving to change myself when God simply wanted me to open up and let him do the changing for me.

As long as I wrestled with the voice which relentlessly insisted—'You must, you must, you must', I was doomed to failure. Only when I was willing for God to enter my life in a new way could I know a deep change from the inside.

Seeking and being found

Derek and I didn't strain ourselves to get better prayer lives. Instead, we opened ourselves up to God completely and asked him to do whatever was necessary to give us a real relationship with himself. He didn't work the way we expected. Before we could be free in our praying, God had to touch us in a very deep way. You'll read about that in chapters eight and nine. For now let me just say that as we opened up our whole lives to God, he took away the chains of indifference and boredom in prayer and showed us what it could be like to meet with Jesus.

Don't misunderstand me. Neither of us just sat back and said to God, 'OK, now you change me.' He could have done that, but he sought our co-operation in his new work in our lives. Too many of us want God to do everything for us. We'll avoid our part and wait for some revelation from heaven to create in us a real relationship with God. It doesn't work that way. The person who truly wants to know God will prove it by the lengths to which he's prepared to go to to discover him. The man who found the pearl of greatest price went out 'looking for fine pearls' (Matthew 13:45). He didn't stay at home and wait for one to fall into his lap! 'You will seek me and find me when you seek me with all your heart', says God in Jeremiah 29:13. And that's a promise.

Let's be Practical

Discipline and persistence

If I asked you to describe the character of the person you know best, you'd talk about the one you've spent most time with. If we're keen to know a deep relationship with God, we'll have to be prepared to meet him regularly. There will be plenty of temptations not to be disciplined. Our past poor experiences of prayer may already have convinced us that prayer may work for others but not for us. We might try it out half-heartedly for a couple of days, expecting all the time to be bored after five minutes. When we try to pray our negative attitude becomes a reality and we give up before we've really started. But praying to Jesus, who is God, shouldn't be tedious. Only when our attitude has been changed from negative to positive can God possibly step in and prove to us that things can be different.

At times it will be hard. Our feelings will tell us that we're getting nowhere and that God isn't listening. On these occasions it's our faith that's being tested. The man who raps only once at his neighbour's door and asks for bread goes home empty-handed. It's only the man who keeps knocking who eventually finds himself being offered all the

bread he wants (Luke 11:1–13). God knows we're going to
have times of struggling. In fact, by giving us this parable,
Jesus warned us that we'd have them. By disciplining
myself and by persevering against all odds, I prove to him
that I'm trusting him not to turn his back on me for ever.
'Blessed is the man who perseveres under trial, because
when he has stood the test, he will receive the crown of life
that God has promised to those who love him' (James 1:12).

A two-way process

God doesn't want clever prayers (Matthew 6:5–13), he
wants a normal conversation with each of his children. He
wants to hear our praise, yes, but also our complaints, our
frustrations, our doubts and fears, our heartaches and
desires and he wants to be allowed to talk to us too. Prayer is
more than 'I speak to God'. It's a two-way process. It's a
shame that there aren't more Christians today who are
sensitive enough to hear God's voice. We begin our quiet
times so concerned about what we want to say that we don't
let him get a word in edgeways.

Specific Prayer

James says, 'You do not have, because you do not ask'
(James 4:2). How easy it is to blame God for allowing
something disastrous to happen when we never bothered to
pray! Similarly, it's all too easy to pray vague prayers and
then to be surprised when we receive only vague answers. If
our motives are pure (James 4:3) and our lives free from
unconfessed sin, then we should *expect* God to answer us
(John 15:7). Let's be specific about our requests and rejoice
as we see definite replies from God.

Large and small requests

If we pray only about major issues (like the conversion of
our families or friends) we'll become very discouraged when
God doesn't seem to be answering our requests. The way to
overcome this is to pray for more immediate matters: a
conversation with a friend tomorrow, the success of an
operation on a church member on Friday, or help for a

Christian group visiting a local prison next week and so on. As God answers these requests, we'll prove that he's listening to us and we'll gain faith to believe that he's working at the bigger issues we're constantly bringing to him. Another advantage in praying for 'short-term' situations is that our prayers will vary from week to week. As a result, prayer should become less boring and we should find ourselves escaping from a ritual and entering into a relationship.

Prayer lists?

Prayer lists can be disastrous! Badly used, they lead us into legalistic routines and shopping-list prayers. When we don't use them at all, we forget to pray for half the things we've promised to pray about. If we change the word 'list' to 'guide' we're on much happier ground. A prayer guide will bring about a certain necessary discipline in our prayers. It will be a flexible reminder of prayer needs rather than a series of items to recite to God each day.

I have a small notebook in which I've written the things I want to pray about. I've marked each page with a number from 1–31 (one for each day of the month). On each day, I've chosen a particular ministry or idea I want to remember. Thus, on the first day of any month, I'll be praying for revival in the Church; on the 6th, for hospital work; on the 9th, for prisons; on the 12th, for Bible translators and so on. Under each heading I've jotted down a few thoughts on the relevant theme and at the bottom of the page I've added the names of three or four friends or well-known Christians. The book is more than thirty-one pages long so at the end of it I've written down the short-term requests for which I pray daily. I'm always adding to these. When I've 'received a reply' to one of them, I cross it off and rejoice! It's true to say that I sometimes fail to pray for the items I've allotted myself on a particular day. But far from feeling guilty, I try to remember that I'm not bound by my notebook and that I have the freedom to pray for totally different things whenever I want to.

There's an art to prayer and the people who discover the

secret are those who are thirsty for a deep fellowship with the Lord. Don't look for prayer without a relationship with God or your prayer life will be stale and legalistic. Seek him. He'll thrill you, guide and help you and he'll delight to reveal to you the depths you can reach in communion with him.

Points to Ponder

1. If your fellowship has a prayer meeting, what are your reasons for attending/not attending it?

2. What do you get out of your prayer meeting?

3. How do you feel about the possibility of some changes being made in the style of those prayer times? (E.g. short praise testimonies, sentence prayers, division of the meeting into smaller prayer groups.)

4. What do you put into your prayer meeting? Should you be contributing more than you do?

5. If asked the question, "What did the Lord teach you in your quiet time today?" would you be embarrassed?

6. Should personal prayer be a duty? Or a pleasure? Can it be both?

7. If you use a prayer list—are your prayer times really a relationship with Jesus or with the prayer list?

8. If you've worked hard at prayer and seem to have got nowhere, might the explanation be that you are not allowing God to provide the inner power to change things?

9. What do you think that 'seeking God with all your heart' really means?

10. How do you react to the following?
    (a) Prayer discipline.
    (b) Persistence in prayer.
    (c) Prayer as a two-way conversation.
    (d) Specific prayer.
    (e) Long- and short-term prayers.
    (f) Prayer lists.

"...ARMED TO THE TEETH WITH PEA-SHOOTERS, WATER-PISTOLS, JEANS AND THICK WOOLLIES."

6

Hot Line to Heaven
Mary

Some time ago, I asked three friends of mine to write down for me how their prayer lives had changed. They're ordinary Christians who have simply opened up their hearts to God. This is what I received:

A middle-aged housewife
'One summer my spiritual and prayer life seemed to have hit rock bottom. I had known the Lord as my personal Saviour for about twenty years and I'd always been actively involved in Christian work. Even so, my prayers (when I made time for them!) only hit the ceiling and few answers seemed forthcoming. I was exhausted with fruitless effort and overwhelmed by all the need. I seemed to have been working in my own strength and leaving the Lord out. I didn't realise that if I only asked, he would given the necessary power to cope with any situation.

The Lord allowed me to be brought very low before him and impressed on me that in my own strength I could do nothing. Gradually, as I asked the Spirit to guide me, he made me more aware of sins in my present and past life. As these were dealt with by confession I began to feel greater liberty in prayer. The 'shopping list' flew out of the window. I enjoyed my time with the Lord and my thoughts wandered less. He now lays a person or circumstance on my heart, making the need clear, so I know I am praying according to his will. To my great joy, most of these prayers are being answered. My appreciation of Scripture has taken on a new dimension too and with it, a realisation that God is a great God who has an endless storehouse of power to work mighty things in my life.'

A young husband

'I had been a Christian for over three years when I was challenged by an older Christian in my church who said "...and God spoke to me saying..." He wasn't talking about the Bible but about his prayer life. I felt rather embarrassed because I had not known until then what it meant to pray in such a way that God joins in as well.

'As a young Christian I had pieced together a few clichés, gleaned from other Christians and constructed my own prayer pattern which would guarantee a few "Amens" if used in public. I prayed broad prayers and received broad answers in return. Then God's Spirit began working in me.

'I could sense God saying to me, "Be honest", and, "Be specific", so I began expressing my true feelings of joy and sadness before the Lord and enjoyed a reverent conversation with him as my Almighty Friend. I would tell God if someone in church was making me angry and ask him to help me. Being more specific in my prayers brought more specific answers and I can now discern on many occasions in prayer what God is saying to me. Prayer is exciting!'

A teenage girl

'It hurts to write this. I suppose that's because it's always hard to expose the worst about yourself, but the truth is that the time each day that I used to spend talking to God was at its best—five minutes; and at its worst—non-existent! That's the bit which hurts because God's changed me. And how did it happen? Well, one particular summer I was crazy about a boy I knew, and yet he just didn't want to know. Whatever subtle means I used had no effect at all. He wouldn't talk to me, or even smile at me—and that cut deep, really deep. I used to come home at night and cry myself to sleep. Then, one night, while I was in the midst of a flurry of tears, God said, "And now do you understand just a little bit of how much you're hurting me? I love you, I really do love you. But you go charging round your little corner of the world, vaguely content with life and totally ignoring me. I don't want ten-second prayers on a Sunday, using all the jargon of the Authorized Version or the cliché phrases you've had rammed down your throat since you could crawl, I want *you*." And now he's got me. Jesus and I have got a really fantastic relationship. No more "Well-here-we-go-God-you've-got-two-minutes-before-I-fall-asleep" affairs; now I wake up in the morning and start talking to him, "Well, what are we going to do today then God?" Prayer is a dialogue now, a real conversation. I sing to him; the words just bubble out of my overflowing heart. And reading the Bible is really exciting because I've got the author right there with me, telling me what it all means. Sometimes, when life hurts too much to talk or when the right words won't come, I just sit on my bedroom floor, silent in his presence, and he's there. Someone once said, "A friend is someone with whom you can be yourself." Love is the operative word. My prayer life changed when I learnt to be myself with Jesus.'

God, Our Friend

When Jesus said to his disciples, 'I no longer call you servants... Instead, I have called you friends' (John 15:15), he was telling them the good news about an exciting new dimension to their relationship with him. He wanted them to see that it was time for them to become his friends as well as his servants. As servants, they'd still be expected to obey him because that would be their duty. But as friends, they'd enjoy a relaxed closeness together, and as a result, they'd do things for him simply because they loved him and wanted to.

Christians are meant to know Jesus on both levels. Sadly, some believers know only a servant relationship with him without establishing a real friendship. They're often dedicated and hardworking people but they're motivated by a sense of duty instead of love. For them, God remains a rather cold and distant figure who gives orders and watches to see if things are done properly.

My friendship with God should somehow resemble my friendship with other people—only it should be richer and deeper. Real friendship is meant to be warm and satisfying, not just 'official'. True friends like to spend time together so they can share their joys and burdens. That's how it should be with God. It's only when I know him in that way that I'll begin to understand what it means to have a real desire to do things that please him. At that point I'll realize I've changed from being just an obedient servant to being God's friend.

Why not?

Why have some Christians never added this other dimension to their relationship with the Lord? Here are some of the reasons:

They may feel that such closeness with God is not primarily what the Christian life is all about. They may have been taught that their main purpose is to get on with serving God. As a result, they're probably so concerned with obedience and service that real fellowship with Jesus is almost completely cut out.

Another common reason why a Christian may not have a deep relationship with Jesus is that he can't believe that Jesus really wants him for a friend. In the past, he may not have had many close companions. They never accepted him, so why should Jesus be any different? Furthermore, if schoolfriends rejected and hurt him, he won't dare risk having the Son of God treat him in the same way. The pain would be too great. So he keeps a safe distance from the friendly hand that Jesus holds out to him.

In addition, some of us find relating to people exceedingly difficult, so we try to avoid human contact by throwing all our energies into 'spending time with Jesus'. We excuse ourselves by maintaining that it's more spiritual to spend time with God rather than people. Unfortunately, this doesn't work. It's impossible to know true friendship with Jesus and yet be isolated from fellowship with human beings. God has made us so that we need both. It's almost impossible for someone who's never had close human friends to relate to the Son of God as his friend. We all need to know companionship on an earthly level to help us to appreciate a heavenly friendship.

Finally, some Christians simply can't be bothered to have Jesus as their friend. They know he offers them daily companionship and love but they're only prepared to go so far with him. There's a limit to their friendship and they refuse to go beyond it.

What a friend we have in Jesus

On the record 'Come Together' there's a song inviting people to open their lives to God. It's really written for unbelievers but the words equally encourage lukewarm Christians to rediscover their neglected friendship with Jesus.

> 'May I introduce you to a friend?
> He's been waiting patiently to meet you.
> A friend on whom you can depend,
> His love will comfort and complete you.
> How long have you been searching
> Groping aimlessly for something
> To fill the emptiness inside
> Someone in whom you can confide?
> Well, he's here waiting for you,
> He's waiting,
> Meet Jesus.'

What kind of friend is he?

Jesus didn't only want his disciples to work for him, he sometimes desired their company alone. 'Come with me by yourselves to a quiet place and get some rest' (Mark 6:31). He must be saying the same words to many Christians today. In his presence I can discover how much he loves me, understands and wants to help me. Unlike even the best of human friends he knows the real 'me' that no one else ever sees. What's more, he accepts me in spite of all the weaknesses and fears that I try to hide from others. Though I may not

understand why, he genuinely wants to enjoy my company—
—whether I'm on Cloud Nine or when my world has
completely caved in.

When I've found the sort of friend who's really interested
in everything I do and think and say, I'll find I want to share
my life with him. Jesus can make my morning quiet times
come alive. I might even discover myself having conversations with him at other times of the day—or maybe in the
supermarket, at the office, over the washing-up bowl or on
walks in the park.

But you say, 'How do I begin to know him better?' In the
past, you may have treated Jesus as a 'God up there' who
popped down to save you and then returned to be with his
Father in heaven. Now start believing that he's here with
you and that he really wants to be your friend. Talk to him
in a simple, natural way. Share with him your fears and
frustrations. He'll listen and he'll solve many of the
problems you may previously have kept to yourself. Your
relationship with him probably won't change overnight. A
human friendship takes time to develop—but it grows as
two people continue to meet and share their lives together.
So it is with God. Your friendship with Jesus can flourish
only when you and he are available to meet each other. He is
always available…

The other side of friendship

Friendship isn't only a happy passive thing where two
people sit or walk about enjoying each other's company.
There's also a very active side to it. Two individuals who are
genuine friends will do things for one another—sometimes
at great cost. The deeper the friendship, the more each one
will sacrifice himself for the wellbeing of the other.

Jesus' friendship with his disciples was often very
one-sided. In Gethsemane just before the crucifixion he
asked his three closest friends to watch and pray, but they
fell asleep. When he needed their support as a mob of armed
men came to arrest him, they all ran away. What's more,
one of them denied him not just once but three times.
Despite all this, Jesus still remained true to them. He went

to the cross and proved by his actions the truth of what he'd earlier said with his lips, 'Greater love has no one than this, that one lay down his life for his friends' (John 15:13).

Jesus' friendship is as reliable today as it was then. But what about us? Some of today's Christians are all mouth and no action—a bit like Peter used to be at times. They're going round saying, 'Lord, Lord' yet they're living for themselves. They prefer to sleep when Jesus calls them to pray. When they face crises in their lives, they run from God's solution because the cost is too high. They try to avoid being noticed as Christians until they're suspected, then they become embarrassed about being called 'religious', laugh it all off and follow the crowd. Yes, even today, Jesus is being deserted by those who are meant to be his closest friends.

God in Command

We each need a balanced relationship with God. In addition to offering us friendship, he also relies on us to fulfil his great commission. For that reason, he enlists us as soldiers in his army. So at times that best friend must become the commanding officer who leads his people into battle.

I often look round at church congregations and wonder how much the people know of the Christian warfare. Are they singing 'Onward Christian Soldiers' simply because it's the next hymn in the service or have they experienced the battle themselves, I wonder? I am impressed by their voices, but are they singing from their hearts?

We love the triumphant songs listed under 'Pilgrimage and Conflict' in our hymn-books but why do so many of us not know personally what it means to fight for God?

'I didn't know!'

Perhaps we didn't know we were supposed to be fighting. Perhaps we don't want to know. It's amazing how much we try to evade challenges. We'll happily pick out all the Bible verses which relate to things we're prepared to do but somehow miss out the ones which will cost us time and effort. If we do find something which threatens to disturb us we're always quick to apply it to someone else instead. (How for instance do we react to the subject of fasting?)

But Jesus battled in prayer. 'He offered up prayers and petitions with loud cries and tears to the one who could save him from death...' (Hebrews 5:7). And Paul speaks of the 'struggle' involved in the Christian warfare (Ephesians 6:12) and attempts to explain the depths of striving prayer: 'The Spirit himself intercedes for us with groans that words cannot express' (Romans 8:26). Countless Christians have found that when they pray they too can enter into fierce combat with Satan. They know what it means to wrestle against the principalities and powers that Paul speaks of. But do we? Or rather, do I?

Paul didn't just want the Romans and Ephesians to know what it was like to stand up against Satan. He wanted today's Christians to enter the warfare too. Satan is the same now as he was in New Testament times, so we must be engaged in exactly the same battle with him as the believers were then. We need the same protection they had, the same power and the same deep experience of prayer.

But all too often we know of none of these things. In our Christian lives we're constantly being defeated and trampled over by the enemy army. We simply don't realise what it's like to confront the devil in prayer, and to see him flee.

'Onward Christian soldiers marching as to war...' we sing. Such hymns of victory emphasise the idea in the Bible that Christians are like soldiers in God's army (Ephesians 6:10–18). Now what soldier in an army never expects to fight? If he didn't plan on being engaged in armed combat, he'd never have signed on in the first place. If I'm meant to be God's soldier I can't possibly spend all my time in the barracks drinking mugs of tea and making friends with the Commanding Officer. There's a battle raging and I've got to be in it.

Now would you say that battles were boring, unemotional and dignified? Never! A battle demands sweat, strain, wrestling, striving, purpose, persevering and deep involvement by every member of the army. The moments of triumph are gained by hours of struggling. It calls for team-spirit and yet individual loyalty. If my prayers never reflect any of this anguish then I never enter the battle at all. I'm just letting others in the Church do the fighting for me.

'Fight whom'?

Once I realise that God wants me to be an active and effective soldier, I've got to get to know the enemy I'm supposed to be fighting. The rebel ranks are described quite vividly in Ephesians 6:12: '...rulers,... authorities... powers of this dark world... spiritual forces of evil in the heavenly realms'. Satan's army is not made up of a band of harmless toy soldiers. The demon hosts are evil and cunning. Satan has thrown all his energies into training them to destroy you. They know your weaknesses. Do you know their strengths?

Satan wants you to believe that you can fight him with pea-shooters and water-pistols. He wants you to think that a pair of tough jeans and a thick sweater will deflect his fiery darts quite effectively. Can you picture God's soldiers turning up to the battle armed to the teeth with pea-shooters, water-pistols, jeans and thick woollies?! That's just about how prepared some of us in today's Church are when it comes to attacking Satan's forces.

But we shouldn't laugh. It's tragic when Christians don't understand the immense power and tactics of the Devil. An army in this situation is in a very sorry state. An individual who doesn't grasp for himself how his greatest foe operates is in an extremely dangerous and vulnerable position. We're faced with the question: 'Would I recognise Satan if I met him?'

Meeting Satan

One of Satan's many disguises is his Angel of Light costume (2 Corinthians 11:14). You may not actually see him, but you'll hear his voice in your mind. He'll find you alone one day, sit down beside you and enter into quiet and apparently sensible conversation. 'Look here,' he'll say, 'there's no need to get over-enthusiastic in your Christian life. That sort of thing's meant for fanatics, not you. Think of what your friends would say if they saw you getting all serious about your religion. You'd put them right off and they'd drop you like a hot brick. Anyway, you don't mean to tell me that you actually believe that rubbish about prayer, do you? Only a person with a brain the size of a pea would think like that! God's given you a life to enjoy, not to spend entombed in some stuffy room on your knees with your Bible. OK, have a quick quiet time in the morning but don't get serious about it or you'll end up being a thorough bore to everyone. Go on out, have a good time, tour the world or something. You'll get to heaven eventually so sit back and relax.'

His direct approach

In his Roaring Lion outfit (1 Peter 5:8), Satan appears in a very different and far more dramatic way. You're sitting cleaning your sword when suddenly over a grass bank not twenty feet away appears a flame-thrower. Then come the accusations: 'You think you're a Christian do you? Well haven't you realised you've committed the unforgiveable sin? You're going to hell to be with me. That situation you're worried about—you can go on worrying because it was all your fault and it's going to get worse... You'll find out before long that you're not going to be able to get through all your work either, in fact, you'll be taking on a bit more than you expected. And it's no good running to your Bible and looking up all those neat promises of God. He doesn't love you so whatever makes you think he'd want to help you out? You're a nobody, you always have been and you always will be.'

Have you ever met him? And if so now have you defended yourself against his attacks? Have you consistently believed his lie that Christianity is nothing more than an effortless faith? Or have you been smashed apart by his accusations and made to feel discouraged, doubtful, guilty, afraid and bewildered? If you don't know him, you'll never be able to resist him. But if you're aware of his evil tactics you'll always be one step ahead.

'Our struggle is not against flesh and blood', the Word of God tells us (Ephesians 6:12). It's against a spiritual enemy. But this enemy is crafty. What he so often does is to divert us from fighting him to squabbling with each other. We actually end up fighting 'against flesh and blood'. He makes us angry and upset over small issues in church so that minor problems become major disasters. Christian unity is destroyed and the fellowship falls apart. While the army of the King is making war on itself, Satan leans back and laughs. When will believers realise what's happening among their own fellowships, get down on their knees and start wrestling against him?

'How do I fight?'

The sort of powerful prayer which defeats Satan doesn't just happen overnight. It can't be 'worked up' any more than you can 'struggle' for a closer friendship with God. Effective, battling prayer emerges naturally as you seek a deeper relationship with Christ. As you come to know him better, he shows you what your enemy is really like and he trains you to fight and defeat him.

God is always looking for believers who don't want just to sing about the Christian warfare but who want to be involved in it. Sadly, the truth is that many of us want our Christianity to be easy. We prefer to remain in the barracks, away from the noise of battle, listening only to joyful Christian music on tapes and avoiding the challenge, agony and excitement of serious striving prayer.

Is it any wonder that we see so few victories in our churches today? When particular prayers are not answered immediately we give up praying altogether and decide that God will sort it out without our help. We don't seem to be prepared to pray much more than two or three times about any difficult situation or problem, let alone fast over it. We'd rather suffer under its weight until the Lord in his kindness eventually lifts it.

But when God places us in hard situations he knows what

he's doing and he's waiting to see our reaction to them. Are we going to give up after offering two or three prayers or go on and, if necessary, become involved in a fierce prayer battle? These can be tremendously moving experiences. They'll build up our faith and help us to see that we really can be 'more than conquerors through him who loved us' (Romans 8:37).

It would be interesting to know how much Christians really do experience of God in their lives. How many could give a fresh and powerful testimony of what he'd been doing over the past two days? How many would be embarrassed if asked to do so? If God is really the friend who walks alongside me and talks to me, then I'll have something to share of what he's been saying. If he's my Commanding Officer who leads me into battle, then I'll have something to share of the fights I've been in. If he isn't really either, then I won't have anything to share at all.

Prayer—an adventure

Prayer is a vast subject. Dozens of books have been written on it and it would be impossible to deal with the entire topic adequately in just two chapters. There are many areas that I haven't touched at all and many that I don't understand. I'm no expert but my appetite for prayer has been whetted by what little I have discovered and I, like others, want to learn more.

It's often the first step that's the hardest. Peter probably thought this when he stepped out of the boat onto the water, but what an experience he had once he had started! A new resolve in prayer is like that. It's difficult to step out of old ways into an adventure in prayer. Fellowship with God won't come overnight, nor without struggles, but it will come —if we're patient. We'll rise and fall in the water as Peter did, but with Jesus there to catch us when we're sinking, there's no better or more exciting place to be.

Points to Ponder

1. When your prayer life isn't all it should be, what are the excuses you tend to use?

2. Do you think that rich prayer times are experienced only by 'special' Christians like pastors, missionaries and evangelists?

3. Can you identify with the 'before' or 'after' of Mary's three friends?

4. How real and close is God? Is he like a distant friend—somebody you keep in touch with?

5. Is it possible to strike up a friendly relationship with God without relating deeply to other Christians?

6. Do you think it's silly to relate to God in everyday situations like peeling the carrots or walking the dog?

7. Do you feel it is rather extreme to suggest that ordinary Christians might engage in spiritual battles?

8. Can you think of recent times when Satan has attacked you while disguised in his 'angel of light' or 'roaring lion' outfit? How did you react?

9. Can you think of times when Satan enjoyed seeing squabbles in your fellowship because Christians were fighting each other instead of him?

10. Could you give a fresh testimony of what God has been doing in your life over the past two days?

"HOW DOES AN ACTOR FEEL WHEN HE'S REMOVED HIS HEAVY COSTUME...?"

7

Operation 'Cover Up'
Mary

Have you ever played the children's card game Happy Families? Each card has a person on it: Mr–, Mrs–, Master–, Miss–. There are about ten different families. Naturally, they are all split up when the cards are dealt to the players and the object is to get as many complete families in your hand as you can. Only then will each family be happy.

We play happy families in church, but in church there should be just one big family and we want the members to relate happily to one another in it. Week after week activities are organised which are supposed to bring us all together: services, prayer meetings, youth clubs, outreach and so on. But do they really unite us?

So often what we call 'fellowship' isn't fellowship at all. It's just 'meeting together'. Derek has a good name for it, he calls it 'Corporate Isolation'. Corporate Isolation is a game played by individuals whose bodies get together at church but whose real selves remain hidden under big Christian smiles. They may belong to the body of Christ but they certainly don't get too close to anyone either physically or emotionally.

Physically Close

With the exception of handshakes the very thought of physical contact between Christians used to send shudders down Derek's spine! You can imagine how he felt then, when one day a Christian man gave him a big embrace! He emerged from it ruffled and very embarrassed! It was all so offensive and unnecessary. He didn't want to be involved in the 'hugs and hallelujah' scene. It was too frivolous, and those who engaged in the touching always seemed slightly over-enthusiastic. It simply was not for him.

Many Christians can identify with this problem. They recall fellowship meetings when a leader has called out 'Now let's all join hands for this chorus', and they have cringed inwardly. When physical contact is forced on people, most of them will do their best to avoid it.

There are many fellowships where touching has become the 'done thing'. The people who belong to them think they are far more 'advanced' than more inhibited Christians who avoid physical closeness. This kind of contact actually puts people off. It's almost a duty, a way of proving to everyone that you're 'liberated'.

But the touch that I want to talk about is not like that. Instead of being an end in itself, it emerges as a natural expression of my love for my fellow Christians. When a mother grasps her child's hand she's saying something. She's speaking in touch.

Only when my touch is motivated by pure love will I know the deep joy that lies behind physical contact. On occasion a hug will be appreciated, but sometimes I may show more love by not touching. I have to learn how to be sensitive to my friends and not to frighten them by an excessive show of affection.

'Jesus reached out his hand and touched the man' (Matthew 8:3)

The touch of Jesus showed much more than just love. It revealed concern, sympathy, support, and identification. I once shared a deep problem with one of my college lecturers. We talked for well over an hour, then the lunch-time bell rang. I joined the other students in the dining-room and stood behind my chair as everyone who hadn't found a place to sit pushed past behind me. The lecturer to whom I'd just been speaking was one of these people. As he passed me, he took hold of my arm and squeezed it gently. No one else would have noticed his action, but in that instant I knew that he understood all the pain I was suffering. He identified with me. He was on my side. He loved me. I could have wept. That little touch meant more to me than the entire conversation I'd had with him.

Some people long to touch others but can't. They're afraid of getting too close. They can't be forced to do it—that simply doesn't work. What they need is to know that they're loved and accepted as they are and to seek for themselves the deep emotional healing which will result in a longing to reach out to others.

Since God has been moving in Derek's life he's changed his mind about this aspect of Christian fellowship. In fact, he rather enjoys it now!

Emotional Closeness

I've talked about sharing myself as a physical person but what about my emotional side? Do I ever share that? How real am I when I'm in company? Do my friends only really know my bright side or do they see me when I'm miserable too?

The church seems to have learnt how to rejoice together but it doesn't know how to weep. Its members do this alone in their homes. Crying in public and letting people see we can't cope are just not acceptable. We embarrass everyone by doing that. We're supposed to tell others how the Lord's been blessing us, but we don't show our weaknesses. In short, it's not right for us to be the people we really are. We have to be the people everyone wants us to be.

The body of Christ should be emotionally linked up. We should be sharing our sadnesses as well as our joys. This doesn't mean that we should all go round complaining and trying to win sympathy from everyone in sight. But we should start being real with one another, admitting we need help at times instead of covering up and battling on alone. I was made to belong to others, to share my life, not to hide it nor to label it: 'Private, No Entry'.

'I don't need you!' (1 Corinthians 12:21)

Many isolated Christians back up their independence by using Scriptures such as Romans 8:37: 'I am more than conqueror through him who loved me'. Others say, 'I just have an independent personality', or, 'I'm trusting the Lord for all my needs. I know I don't get very close to people, but that's the way I am. I simply prefer to work on my own.' These are the people who find it hard, if not almost impossible, to go to other Christians for help. They've always been able to cope and they believe they should continue to manage alone. Indeed, they believe God wants them to. But is this really true?

God wants no such thing! Did you notice the mis-quotation of Romans 8:37? What the verse actually says is not, 'I am more than conqueror,' but *'We* are more than conquerors.' The whole thing is plural. Soldiers don't fight battles and win victories alone and Christians don't either. There will be times of course, when we have to make our own personal stand, but we are called to belong to a body, so if I declare, 'I can manage alone', I'm inventing my own verse and I'm fooling myself when I think that I don't need others to support me.

Believers who insist on staying apart from people generally lead a very lonely life. They may not admit this to others or even to themselves but underneath they cry out for the warmth and affection that their friends can give. But they can't let it show. They've gained a reputation for being 'strong' and so cannot let the mask slip and show weakness. They've trapped themselves into staying the way other people expect them to be.

But suppose they knew?

It's not only independent people who live behind false smiles. Haven't you ever felt that no one really understands you? There are friends you see and joke with and yet you've never shared with them the real you. On the outside you display a mask of happiness but on the inside you're often feeling weak, insecure and lonely. Do you laugh at those who are willing to admit to their sadness when really you suffer in the same way yourself? You just cover it up because you're afraid that if you let anyone know your true self you'll be rejected.

So you live up to expectations and wear the same happy smile that everyone else does. We all blind ourselves to our insecurities, our weaknesses and humanity. We meet together to praise God that we are one body in Christ and each of us comes away with the thought, 'Nobody understands me'. That's not surprising if we've never allowed anyone to know us in the first place.

Time to pause

'Get a move on! Step on it! Hurry!' The modern world is continually forcing us on. We're pressurised to strive for higher and higher standards, to keep up with the latest fashions, to go, go, go! We daren't stop or we'll be left behind.

The same is true of Christians. How frequently we hear sermons about moving on. 'Forget what lies behind! Look to Jesus! Battle on! Claim the victory!' But soldiers who are always fighting will become tired and useless if they don't stop sometime. Now and again Christians need to pull out, sit down and think hard. They need to question: 'Am I the effective Christian that I think I am?'

Self-examination is not something most of us enjoy. In fact, more often than not, we try to find as many excuses as possible why we shouldn't take a long, hard look at our lives. The simple truth is that we don't want to. We're happy the way we are. We don't want to conduct a thorough self-examination because we'd rather not know about anything which may be wrong in us. So we hide from the possibility that there might be something. We throw ourselves into all sorts of activities so that we don't get the chance to think too hard about our Christian walk. We repeat all the Scriptures which speak of pressing onward and dodge the ones which challenge us to stop and reflect: 'See if there is any offensive way in me' (Psalm 139:24).

The Apostle Peter was a real extrovert. He was the natural leader of the twelve, always full of energy and often making mistakes. He bubbled with activity and radiated self-confidence. He was a man who thought he knew himself, and he made the boldest of claims to prove his manly character. 'Even if all fall away on account of you, I never will... Even if I have to die with you, I will never disown you' (Matthew 26:33,35).

When the time of testing came—what happened? Peter fled from Gethsemane with all the others and then in the courtyard he cursed and swore that he'd never been with Jesus.

Poor Peter. All he could see were his strengths. But he really wasn't the rock he thought he was. Underneath, he was a coward. Jesus faced him with his true nature, his mask slipped and he realised who he actually was. Shattered by the truth about himself, he went out and wept bitterly.

Afraid of truth

Many believers—pastors and church leaders included—have never allowed God to unmask them. They go around thinking they've achieved effective Christian lives when in fact the reverse is true. They say they know they're weak but they've never really been to Gethsemane and the courtyard with Peter and had it proved. They've often hidden away their insecurities and fears for so long that they, like Peter, wouldn't recognise themselves if these anxieties ever came out into the open. Often these are the people who are continually calling for Christians to 'press on' and be victorious. They do it because they themselves are too frightened or threatened by the thought of stopping and thinking about their own identities.

Every Christian ought to be willing to be tested like Peter, but few of us are open to the challenge. Why is this? The simple and honest reason is that it hurts. If I don't look too deeply at my life I can avoid the pain which will come to me if I spend time getting to know myself. To allow God to unpeel the protective layers I've applied over the years is going to cause me distress. I don't want to know I'm unhappy inside so I escape and refuse to look. I give myself excellent excuses why it's wrong for me to conduct any thorough self-examination.

But the longer we hold out against allowing God to open us up, the longer the whole Church is going to suffer from Corporate Isolation. If we continue to hide our real selves and cover up our faults we're never going to be able to relate closely at all. Every time we're together, my mask will simply go on meeting yours. It's time we learnt how to stop pretending to be happy when we're not. It's time we learnt to be real.

Accept the challenge

'Do you know who you are?' I can't challenge you personally with this question. But you can challenge yourself if you honestly want to know the answer. If you're really open, you won't worry about the test described below. If you're hiding behind a mask, you won't like it at all. Here's your chance to prove to yourself that you are real.

Find three Christians outside your family who know you well and whom you can trust. Meet each of them separately and ask them to give you an honest description of what they think you're like. Don't pick individuals who are going to tell you things you want to hear. Rather choose those whose opinions you'll value, those who, in love, will tell you both what you want to know and what you don't. Take note of what they say, then go away and think hard about it. Take your friends' views seriously. Are you really the person you thought you were?

'Surely,' you may say, 'there's a real danger of becoming self-centred'. I wouldn't disagree with that but from what I've seen in churches, the opposite danger is more likely. We concern ourselves with everyone else and simply don't examine our own lives enough. God doesn't want people who are continually pretending to love each other, he wants the real thing. He doesn't want to see individuals going round sharing only their spiritual revelations. He wants genuine human beings who are going to be honest about their doubts and fears. He wants people who know not so much how strong they are but how weak, because only those who recognise their weakness know that they need his power and his family to lean on.

But be warned. Although discovering who you are underneath is a rewarding experience it is also a painful one and it shouldn't be treated lightly. Being willing to talk to three individuals about yourself is only really the beginning. God wants you to go on and face yourself before he will lay his healing hand on your life. That often means confessing to all sorts of things about yourself you'd rather no one knew about. God wants his children to be real, but there's a price to be paid and you need to have people around who will love and support you throughout.

What happens?

How does an actor feel when he's removed his heavy costume and the thick make-up he's had plastered all over his face? Free! He'll walk out of his hot stuffy dressing-room into the cool night air and he'll rejoice that he doesn't always have to be somebody he's not. He can be himself instead.

That's how it feels when you've got nothing to hide, when you've hung up your mask and decided that you're never going to wear it again. The process of removing it may be hard but the joy and release that follow are great.

The most wonderful things would happen if everyone in my church decided to become real. Bit by bit we could open up our lives to each other. Your little step forward would encourage me to take another one. The more I learnt to accept you, the more you'd want to do the same for me. We'd begin to work together in a new way, sharing richer, deeper fellowship and drawing closer as a body than ever before. There would be great joy, love and freedom in a community like that. There'd be no playing games any more. We'd all belong to a genuine Happy Family.

Points to Ponder

1. Do you take part in the 'corporate isolation' game by hiding your real self behind a Christian smile?

2. What do you feel about a careful and discreet use of touch in Christian relationships?
   (a) Can you recall instances where touch has been helpful to you?
   (b) Do you think it is helpful to many people?
   (c) Should we use touch more than we do?
   (d) What about people who simply don't want to be touched?

3. To what extent are you able to share the joys or sorrows of other people?

4. What do you think of the argument that Christians should learn to cope alone because leaning on others is a sign of weakness?

5. Within your own fellowship, do you think that people would actually be rejected if they removed their masks?

6. How do you think your church would benefit if more people took off their masks? Or would it not be helpful at all?

7. Do you think that an honest self-assessment would benefit you? Could this be done without the risk of becoming too morbid about it?

8. What do you think is the best way of going about this? Would it help to ask three friends for their opinions about you?

"DEREK WAS SURROUNDED BY CHRISTIANS WHO HAD A REAL RELATIONSHIP WITH GOD...."

8

Derek's Escape
Mary

The Jews of Jesus' time had very definite ideas about their religious lives. Although some were hypocritical, many were genuinely trying to please God. The trouble was that they were going about it in the wrong way because they had misunderstood what God wanted. Instead of bringing them freedom, their religion had brought them into a miserable bondage and what is worse, they didn't even know it.

The same is true today. There are thousands of real Christians whose lives lack joy and power because they cling to wrong ideas of how the Christian life should be lived. They are totally unaware that anything is wrong so they struggle on year after year thinking that theirs is normal Christianity.

'Christianity is not an emotional faith'

Derek once thought he knew how the Christian life should be lived. His Christianity was cold and logical. You committed yourself to Jesus Christ and then with God's occasional help, you tried to lead a good life. God would be somewhere in the background but certainly not as close as some people claimed he could be. If you went to church twice a week and did a little witnessing then God would be pleased.

To him, Christianity was not an emotional faith at all and people who claimed to have 'spiritual experiences' were overenthusiastic and even unbiblical. Derek firmly believed that prophecies, tongues and anything remotely 'out of the ordinary' should be totally avoided. These things were frightening and divided churches. God was a God of order and peace, and Christians should not seek 'extra experiences'. It would be better for them to 'come down to earth' and build solid foundations.

Derek had achieved a great deal in his twenty years as a Christian and he had done it without any extraordinary 'blessings' of any kind. He had preached three hundred times and had co-founded five churches in the USA and one in Great Britain. He had built up Moorlands Bible College from twenty-six students in 1970 to eighty-three in 1980. What's more, he had written three Christian books, the last of which had become a best seller. He was evidently a man who, when it came to the Christian life, knew what he was talking about.

At Moorlands, Derek naturally avoided associating too much with the 'charismatic crowd' and tried to maintain a 'respectable' image. He had to because he was an elder in a local church and often received invitations to preach to other congregations. His messages were generally very acceptable because of the hard work he put into preparing them. He was quite an easy-going, approachable sort of person, yet he remained correctly detached from the students. He felt that it wasn't good to get too close to people—particularly during counselling sessions.

Derek wasn't concerned about the brevity of his 'quiet times' (when he had them). What really excited him was the work that God had given him to do—and that couldn't have been more successful. He was still in his thirties. He had a PhD in Chemistry, had published more than twenty major scientific papers and was now a church-planter, author and Bible College principal. There was no doubt that God was with him—everything he did flourished. He had a bright future ahead too. What more could there be in the Christian life? How could anyone serve God more faithfully? Surely Derek had found the key to the most satisfying Christian experience.

A weak leader

You'd think that the principal of a Bible College would command the respect and admiration of those he worked with and taught. However, in spite of his impressive achievements and his dedicated hard work, a large number of the college students looked down on him. Why was this?

Maybe one of his problems was his physical appearance. He was tall and on the thin side and to be honest, he just looked weak. He also had an unconscious nervous habit of raising and lowering his shoulders—particularly when he was addressing the student body. This unfortunate mannerism was frequently used by people who wanted to impersonate him. His wide, colourful ties didn't help him to gain admiration either. Derek thought they made him like 'one of the students' but we got the impression that he was trying to be someone he just wasn't. He was trying to project an image which would make him popular.

Yet Derek's real problem wasn't so much his physical appearance but something else: he simply longed to be accepted, and day after day he was attempting to win the love and support of everyone. He did all he could think of to be liked. He tried to joke with the students and sometimes even acted the fool to gain attention. All the time he avoided offending anybody because he couldn't bear the thought of rejection. Even his sermons at college fell on deaf ears and made little impact. He was afraid of saying something offensive and so steered a safe, dull course through each of his messages. One morning he found a note pinned to his study door. It read: 'You can please some of the people some of the time, but you can't please all of the people all of the time.' The student who wrote it was one of the many who saw a weak leader who couldn't stand up for himself and express his own definite opinions.

Emotional chains

It's easy to criticise those you don't understand. We students were well aware of Derek's weaknesses without really knowing the reason why. The fact is that many unhappy incidents which happened in his childhood were haunting him. He had locked these painful events inside himself and even though several decades had gone by, he was still suffering from them and struggling to cover them up.

'During my childhood I was in very poor health. I suppose I might have been described as "sickly". I remember one occasion when snow had to be brought into the house on a tray because I was too ill to play outside with the other children. Later, when the other boys were joining Boy Scouts, I couldn't because I was too ill and frail.

'By nature I was rather shy and timid. Most adults treated me sympathetically but not the youngsters at school. They seemed to despise me for my feebleness. When it came to anything remotely rough or daring, I was definitely not one of the 'gang'. I was the kind of child who got bullied but I never showed how much I was hurting until I came home to mummy. Other children didn't seem to want my friendship. A boy called Peter was the only one who seemed to accept me and he died suddenly one day of broncho-pneumonia. I missed him deeply.

'Covering up my fears and weaknesses had become a habit by the time I was seven. On one Sunday School outing I had only 15p to spend at the funfair and each 'go' cost 3p. I was desperately afraid of losing my reputation with the small group chosen to go around together, so whatever they chose to do, I did too. I really wanted to try other things but fear had taught me to fit in with the opinions and decisions of others in case I fell out of favour.

'Not all my teachers were helpful to me. One of them continually scolded and even struck me on several occasions because my head leaned somewhat towards my right shoulder. This wasn't my fault and I eventually had surgery to correct it. Another teacher knocked me about in front of the whole school because one or two of us had booed as the small choir sang. At the time I had no idea that I was doing wrong—it just seemed funny.

'The total effect of the first eleven years of my life was that I entered adolescence with a strong sense of injustice and personal rejection. My health improved greatly, but not my relationships. I had almost no friends, although I did manage to team up with another loner who had a similar interest in stamp collecting. By the time I reached the sixth form, I was throwing all my weight into my studies. While the other chaps talked about their daring exploits, I just got on with my work. I was glad to be accepted academically, but on the personal side, I felt very inferior. I was convinced that no one really liked me or would be in the least interested in listening to what I had to say.'

It was against this background that Derek left for university—academically able but personally weak, immature and insecure. On his very first evening away from home he was introduced to Jesus Christ and accepted him as Saviour and Lord. Becoming a Christian was a real turning point. Derek began to feel accepted by other believers and was astounded that they should actually like him. But still inside him lurked the idea that he couldn't be fully appreciated as he was. He had to prove he was worthy of love. He had to win it. Even becoming a husband and a father seemed to make very little difference to the feeling of inferiority.

Years later, as principal of Moorlands, Derek was still struggling to gain the friends he had never had before but he was still failing. The past was simply repeating itself and he still felt despised and rejected by most people.

Spiritual chains

God treats us as individuals. No two people have exactly the same needs. Strangely, God didn't want to sort out Derek's emotions first of all. He was more concerned with something else and that was his spiritual life. Although Derek knew much about Christianity, he knew almost nothing of a day-to-day relationship with Jesus. He was a Christian, but his faith was cold and God was a remote figure who wasn't meant to be particularly close—or was he?

'Although I didn't want to admit it, the very Christians I was criticising seemed to have a surprisingly powerful and satifying faith. Suppose they were genuine? Suppose that what they said was true and God really did reveal himself in what I regarded as extraordinary ways? These ideas were too challenging for me to face. For if they were true then I'd have to admit to myself that my own relationship with God needed a great deal of attention. To be frank, I didn't really want to know that there was any better Christianity than the variety I already had. So I escaped the challenge and tried to tell myself that those who had unusual experiences were somewhat unbalanced.'

But many of them weren't unbalanced, and their presence was beginning to make Derek feel rather uncomfortable. Some of those Christians really did have a vital relationship with God and he couldn't deny it. Surely he, a church founder, an author, a Bible College principal had the key to a victorious Christian life and yet increasingly he was battling with the knowledge that he hadn't. For a long time he refused to look honestly at his relationship with the Lord. He couldn't face the truth about the poor quality of his quiet times. He dared not admit that the Bible was dull and uninteresting or that his prayers lasted about three minutes each day. After all, Derek was a Christian leader and Christian leaders just do not confess that their spiritual lives are in a complete mess.

Eventually, God managed to break through. Derek was surrounded by Christians who had a real relationship with God, and he could no longer doubt their sincerity. They spoke as if they knew their Lord and he shone through their lives. Derek's feeble spiritual experience was put to shame by their testimonies of God's love and power. Reluctantly, he turned from his long-held belief that Christians cannot have further dramatic spiritual experiences after conversion and he found that his whole life began to change.

When the chains fall off

There were no blinding flashes or sensational events to shake Derek out of his old Christian ways. In fact, the change was so gradual that it would be difficult to pinpoint exactly when it all came about. God simply opened his eyes to an entirely new dimension of Christianity. Derek saw a God who cared for him and who didn't just demand to be served but who desired to be his friend.

As time went on, Derek realised how much God wanted to be involved in his life—even in small things. He started to expect the Lord to do things for him and his quiet times not only came back into existence, they came alive as well. The Bible, which had been a dead book for so long, began to speak to him and he discovered that he could actually enjoy praying. A distant Lord was rapidly becoming a close companion who wanted to help Derek in everything he did. Derek was at last beginning to understand and experience the abundant life that Jesus offered him.

As Derek allowed God to be involved in his life, he discovered that he was naturally becoming emotionally stronger. God accepted him with all his weaknesses so there was no longer any need to try to be 'somebody'. Derek relaxed and let God transform him from within. He gave up struggling to be liked and started to relate to everyone in a much more natural and positive way. His whole ministry took on a new turn. Charged with a real love for people, he started to involve himself in their problems to a greater degree than ever before. His pulpit ministry changed too. It had a new authority which had never been evident in the past. He even stopped wearing those appalling picture ties! Perhaps for the first time in his life, he had begun to be himself.

A real work of God in a person's life doesn't need to be spoken about, it's seen. Derek didn't go around proclaiming he had been changed. He didn't need to—people could tell there was something different about him. Some of them even went up to him and told him that they could see the change. Let Derek have the last word:

'I've changed so much in the last few years. I'm more free now than I've ever been. My spiritual life is almost totally different. God is so real that sometimes I can almost touch him and the Bible has become like a new book to me. I'm beginning to enjoy some of the power that Jesus promised. Emotionally I'm much more relaxed and able to be myself. I still get hurt fairly easily but I'm handling it more honestly. Sometimes that old sense of rejection comes back, but it matters less and less as I experience more of my total acceptance by God himself.

God has removed the heaviest and rustiest spiritual and emotional chains from my hands and feet. Now I can enjoy the glorious world of New Testament Christianity which I'd known so little about during my first twenty years as a Christian. I've a long way to go yet, but like Paul, 'I press on to take hold of that for which Christ Jesus took hold of me' (Philippians 3:12).

Points to Ponder

1. How can we find out if we have the wrong ideas of what Christianity really is?

2. Is the following statement true in your life: 'You committed yourself to Jesus Christ and then, with God's occasional help, you tried to lead a good life'? (p. 87)

3. Is it right to measure success in terms of achievement rather than the depth of our relationship to God?

4. What stops us from following the example of those who obviously have a deeper relationship with God than we do?

5. How real is the risk of rejection if we dare to be ourselves in front of others?

6. What steps should a Christian take who realises that his Christian life is in a mess?

"SHE WAS SEEN TO BE SOME SORT OF SUPER-CHRISTIAN....?"

9

Mary's Escape
Derek

I first met Mary in the hot, dry summer of 1976 when she came to Moorlands for an informal interview. Although she'd been a Christian for only two years, she spoke confidently about her relationship with God and about his power in her life. My first impressions were that Christ meant everything to her. Following her official interview a few weeks later, she was accepted as a student.

'Christ is the answer'

During her first year at college it seemed that those impressions of mine were correct. Mary's commitment to Christ was one hundred per cent. While some girls spent their time chasing the fellows, she devoted her energies to prayer and fasting. She spent so much time in God's presence that she rarely took part in the everyday things of college life like volleyball or chatting over coffee in the lounge. If ever a person practised self-denial it was Mary. It was clear from her lack of new clothes that she didn't often spend money on herself.

Her face was nothing short of radiant and her bright expression never dropped even for a moment. Minor things may have troubled her now and again but she never became seriously unhappy. She found it hard to understand when fellow students sometimes became depressed or irritable. Everyone had her on a pedestal all right, and for good reason—she was as close to God as one could possibly be.

One day, as a group of us were sipping tea, I asked her point blank, 'How do you always manage to look so radiant?' 'Oh, it's the Lord', she replied and I knew she was right—how else could a Christian be continually victorious?

Mary genuinely believed that all Christians should be triumphant over their emotional lives. How could anybody be a really faithful servant of God and yet suffer at the same time from depression? There were only two alternatives: 'victorious believer' or 'defeated unbeliever'. No compromise was possible. After all, the Bible spoke of being 'more than conqueror' (Romans 8:37) and of being able to do 'everything through him (Christ) who gives me strength' (Philippians 4:13). To believe these Scriptures made it impossible for a Christian to have any deep depressing problems. Rather than dishonour the Lord and make him out to be a liar, Mary chose to live victoriously, proving to other believers that in Christ she had discovered the solution to all depression.

Living a lie

After a year and a half at college, things quite suddenly started to go wrong. In May 1978, Graham Kendrick came to Moorlands to talk to the students about music in evangelism and words from one of his songs hit Mary hard. By the time he'd reached the fourth verse there was a lump at the back of her throat.

> 'Please excuse me,
> I've spent so many lonely years
> Locked up inside me
> Behind the door which through the years
> Was closed to keep outside the fears
> I've known when life just seemed
> To make me stand alone
> I'm rediscovering my true feelings.'

She left the room fighting back the tears.

We all think we know who we are and so long as no one tells us anything about ourselves that we don't like, we're quite happy. But what happens when someone comes up and points out a fault in us we'd never realised was there? At first, we're surprised, then threatened and then probably hurt and resentful. When that person has gone, we react in one of two ways. Either we ignore what was said and try to forget it, or we begin to investigate whether or not it's true. So when God effectively tapped Mary on the shoulder and whispered, 'Mary, your whole Christian life is one big lie', she just couldn't believe what she was hearing. But after her initial protests ('Look at my devotion to you! Everyone knows how committed I am!'), she began to think.

Behind that superspiritual smile what was she genuinely like? No one at college really knew and, strange to say, she didn't either. Unconsciously she'd always resisted knowing her true self and had fought off any distressing thoughts about what she was actually like. All she wanted to believe was that she was a faithful and devoted servant. Then God began to show her just how mistaken she was.

Emotional chains

'God forced me to see all the things about myself that I'd never wanted to know and then he showed me how I'd come to be the person I was. Throughout my childhood and teenage years I had almost no self-confidence at all. I covered up my weaknesses by avoiding close relationships with my classmates. "Independence is strength" became my motto and I tried to prove to everyone, including myself, that I could live much better without people. During lessons I rarely spoke up in case my opinions were crushed, which would have made me feel even more inferior. In the end I considered my opinions so worthless that I almost stopped having them at all—in that way I could never be wrong. My real achievements were few and far between and in my desperation to prove that I could do at least some things well, I became quite expert at cheating in tests and examinations.

'At break time I seldom joined my friends in their games and not surprisingly they decided that I was unfriendly. As they didn't invite me to play with them I spent more and more time on my own and convinced myself that I didn't care whether they wanted me with them or not. That way my weakness would be seen as strength. But underneath I cared deeply and inwardly I cried out for acceptance and love.'

As she learnt how to deny all feeling of weakness, Mary gradually forgot what it was like to desire help and to depend on others. Slowly she began to lose her humanity and tenderness and to replace them with hardness. The more she isolated herself from people, the less she knew how to relate to them. The less she knew how to relate to them, the more she avoided them. It was a vicious circle. In time, Mary became nothing much more than a feelingless blob—physically podgy and emotionally cut off from the real world.

When she became a Christian and experienced the infilling of God's power at the same time, the change was tremendous, and for several weeks she went about telling everyone how wonderful Jesus was. Then she settled down to enjoy her new-found freedom. But, although she didn't realise it at the time, she wasn't free. Spiritually she had been changed by God, but emotionally she was the same independent and unemotional person she'd always been. She was simply living her new life in the old shell.

At Moorlands she took care to avoid close contact with people. She found an excellent excuse. Instead of spending time with student friends she'd slip off to her room to talk to God. It was a perfect escape route. The Lord would be pleased with her devotion and Mary would manage to remain independent. At the same time, people would be impressed by her holiness.

But the holiness was a sham. Mary was simply afraid of people. One basic problem was that she really didn't think anyone wanted her as a friend. She was convinced that she'd be more of a nuisance to others than anything else. Besides, closeness might involve criticism and she didn't want to be criticised. She didn't want to be laughed at, and she didn't want to be left out. Deliberately she chose to isolate herself before anyone had the chance to reject her.

However, by using this means of hiding, Mary was at the same time gaining an image. Because she was alone with God so much, she was seen to be some sort of super-Christian. Suddenly Mary found that she was having to live up to what others expected of her and in time she began to hate the idea that others thought she was really holy. But she couldn't escape it. To do so would mean to let God down. Anyway, the very notion that she could possibly be a fearful, unhappy Christian was more than she could bear. She repressed the thought as best she could and continued to live in her unreal world, depending on nobody, with nobody depending on her.

When God broke into her isolation and showed her who she was, Mary's conviction that Christians could never suffer from depression suddenly disappeared for now she had begun to experience the deep unhappiness she'd condemned others for having. Her problem didn't have a 'spiritual' answer because it wasn't a 'spiritual' problem in the first place. The trouble lay deep in Mary's emotions. She was imprisoned by her past choices and experiences. As a result, her present relationship with Jesus was suffering.

Spiritual chains

'What people thought they saw in me was a supreme dedication to God. What they never knew was that God was about as far away from me as the man in the moon. I thought that because I was a charismatic Christian I couldn't be troubled by emotional or spiritual problems but although I was thrilled with the experience of God's power, my inner spiritual life was anything but joyful. Instead of relaxing in the presence of a warm and loving heavenly Father, I was obsessed with attempting to placate and satisfy a God who always seemed to be frowning and waving a big stick at me. So I spent much of my time ruthlessly rooting out all kinds of sins, hoping that somehow God would be pleased with me and begin to smile at me. But he never did, and my striving for perfection gradually became a dull and legalistic routine. All those hours of praying and days of fasting didn't spring from a free and happy relationship with a heavenly Father but were more in the nature of good works for a hard-to-please God. To put it in a nutshell—I was in bondage and my Christianity was miserable.!

What could she do to escape? The answer didn't lie in 'spiritual' pursuits. She could scarcely have been more devoted to Jesus. She was already doing everything she could think of to be right with him. What was needed was an emotional change. Mary had to become aware of who she really was. Then she had to learn to accept herself just as God did.

When the chains fall off

God himself revealed to Mary that her Christian life was in a mess but that didn't solve anything. Self-understanding is one thing, but release is quite another. A prisoner in a dark dungeon may have no problem believing that he's in bondage, he wants to know how to get free. That freedom began for Mary only when she swallowed her pride and went to her college tutor for help. It took courage, but she knew she had to talk to someone because God had begun to tear her life apart and she just had to have somebody there to lean on. Looking back, she can see now how that first counselling session was one of the major keys to her emotional release. Once her hidden sorrows were known and understood by one person, there just didn't seem to be any need to hide them from anyone else any more. Little by little the superspiritual mask fell away and she gently re-entered the world of people.

Mary's independence didn't suddenly disappear overnight. At first it was all strange. After a lifetime of avoiding people it was hard to relate to them and she often felt awkward in company. She was shocked to learn that she had emotions and could hardly come to terms with her new and often sinful feelings. She 'knew' she wasn't like this. But as it dawned on her that she was a human being, she steadily began to change.

She realised that however incredible it might seem, other Christians were equally human. They shared her doubts, fears and insecurities. She could actually understand them. As she started to relate to them she shared her experiences and they began to see that Mary was a real person after all. What joy! She felt like the prodigal daughter returning home from a miserable pigsty. Christians actually welcomed, accepted and loved her without her mask and she really enjoyed being with them.

As she became more honest with herself and with people, so she realised that her relationship with God was changing. Her efforts to please a judgmental and tyrannical Lord collapsed and God showed her that he was her friend. He loved her. She could talk to him in a natural way and he'd listen and answer her. She could actually enjoy being with him.

Mary was thrilled when a Christian friend said to her, 'Mary, the thing I like about you is that you're real.' The change in her is by no means complete but (as she says) the major operation has been performed and future surgery will hopefully be less drastic and less painful too.

'At last I'm discovering a joyful faith. That old tense relationship with a distant almighty Lord is slipping away and I find I'm beginning to relax with Jesus and enjoy him. I'm spending much more time with people too and I think I'm learning how to love them. I still find it difficult to express my feelings in words and to allow other Christians to help me. God and I will just have to work on those together in the future. The final verse of Graham Kendrick's song sums up the beautiful change that God has brought about in my life.'

> 'But my confidence in friends is really growing
> And I'm not half so scared to make my feelings known
> I know that even when I'm wrong
> His love still stands, it's really strong
> Now I can laugh and I can cry and I can sing
> The sweetest joys and saddest tears can now begin
> An honest heart and honest eyes
> It's been a beautiful surprise
> Since God gave me my true feelings.'

And the truth will set you free

There must be thousands of emotionally unhappy Christians. They've kept their fears to themselves and even *from* themselves. Inside they're crying out for help. There must be thousands of spiritually miserable Christians. They use a great deal of energy escaping from the truth that their relationship with God is sad, impersonal—but inside they long to be like others who have a really vital faith.

We know what it's cost us to be honest with ourselves. We've been through real agony to discover the truth about our lives. We've had to face up to things we didn't want to see and confess sins we never realised we had. But what about the result? We've found freedom! The freedom that comes through not having to live up to what others want us to be. The freedom that comes in knowing that we're accepted and loved as we are. The freedom to be ourselves.

> 'If you hold to my teaching, you are really my
> disciples. Then you will know the truth, and the
> truth will set you free' (John 8:31,32).

Points to Ponder

1. What happens to a Christian who believes that he must never feel depressed or be defeated?

2. How do most of us react when we are told an unpleasant truth about ourselves?
   (a) Reject it and become angry?
   (b) Feel hurt inside but say nothing?
   (c) Admit that it's true and seek to put it right?

3. What are the advantages and disadvantages of the 'Independence is strength' idea?

4. When people are afraid of close relationships, what kinds of cover do they often hide behind?

5. Once we get away from the extreme of treating God as harsh and tyrannical, is there a danger of regarding him merely as an easy-going friend?

6. What can a Christian do who has become isolated from fellowship with other believers?

"A YOUNG PRINCESS BY ACCIDENT DROPPED HER FAVOURITE TOY — A GOLDEN BALL — INTO A POOL OF WATER."

10

Bind Us Together Lord
Derek

'Thank you Lord for this wonderful time of fellowship we've had together.'
Along with the rest of the congregation I quietly whispered, 'Amen.' I'd said 'Amen' to this kind of prayer many times before. Somehow on this particular occasion in 1977 things didn't seem right. I was uneasy because I actually began to think about what had been prayed.

'Fellowship...together' I pondered.
'With whom have we had fellowship and to what depth?' I wondered. I had certainly enjoyed fellowship with God because he had been very close and real to me in that service. Then I thought about the other ninety-nine people in the church. They had probably enjoyed God's presence too. But had they experienced any fellowship with each other? Or with me?

No, they hadn't, I realised. My eyes may have met someone else's occasionally, and my hand may have accidentally touched another as we passed the collection bag. I'd said, 'Good morning', to several people before the service began, and one or two folks had asked me how I was. I'd given the polite reply, 'Fine, thank you.'

Love God—love his family

That was about all. It was dignified and correct yet it was so shallow. I felt as though no one cared about me enough to want a deeper conversation. I didn't really care much about them either. It was all very sad—not a bit like the early church described in Acts.

Until then, for me fellowship meant attending a service, sitting and standing alternately between hymns and other items, chatting briefly afterwards, then going home. For years I hadn't expected anything different—I'd been content with this meagre ration of fellowship.

Then God began to change me. He became much more real to me. At the same time, as God and I became closer, I found that I wanted deeper relationships with my fellow Christians too. I was beginning to love them and I wanted us all to be more involved in each others' lives.

Then came some of the problems. One or two friends told me I was wrong in my desire to get close to people. 'You mustn't care so much about people—it's not good for them or you. You'll trust one another rather than the Lord,' I was told. I struggled inwardly as I saw a conflict between these criticisms and my growing affection for my Christian friends. Ought I to feel guilty about my new outlook? Was I really beginning to trust people rather than God? Was I backsliding?

I decided to question God about it, and to search the Scriptures for the answers. I was happy to find that backsliding wasn't my problem because my appreciation of God was increasing week by week. When I turned to the Bible I was comforted to discover that my new outlook was biblical after all. God *did* intend us to be close to each other. I was not backsliding, I was growing!

I must be honest and admit that closeness does have its dangers. We can become too attached to one another and replace God by Christian fellowship. There's meant to be a balance between the two. We aren't supposed to be isolated either from God or from his people. We are to rely on God alone, and at the same time, to trust him *through* our relationships and not *instead* of them.

Some Christians have swung too far on the people side and away from God. Others have very shallow relationships with people. Often they are not very close to God either. Theirs is a lonely existence because they don't feel near to God or to members of his earthly family.

What unites us?

When we serve God together in a joint project we rightly call ourselves 'co-workers'. It's really good to be with a group of people dedicated to a particular task like door-to-door visitation or Sunday School teaching. But what is it that holds us together? Is it our common relationship with Christ? Or is it the project? It's both, yet there ought to be something else too.

That extra something is the relationship we have with each other as people. We may picture it something like this:-

Held together only by Christ and by the tasks we do.

United also by our involvement with each other because we are members of God's family.

God intends us to love and care for each other on the human as well as on the spiritual level. Genuine and deep friendship is normal not sinful.

On the practical day to day level most of us see our relationships only in terms of what we do together (like attending a service or planning a camp reunion). Having completed the job in hand we think we've had 'fellowship' with each other. But to what extent have we really been open to one another as we worked? Probably very little. We are more geared up to the project itself than to personal involvement with people. It's the task alone that matters to each of us.

Mary and I have spent hundreds of hours together working on this book. Most of the time we've enjoyed it because both of us have felt enthusiastic about it. Yet the book isn't our total relationship. We have much more in common that a manuscript. We're genuinely close friends too, and that's much more important. In fact the writing came as a result of our relationship, and even though the work's now finished we're as close as before.

Suppose your prayer group or youth work committee suddenly disbanded, what would be left of your relationship with the other members? If your answer is, 'Well, not much', then you can be sure that there's something missing—real fellowship.

I must admit, at times I value the job I'm doing with someone more than the person I'm doing it with. When we're not talking about the work we're doing we have very little else to say to each other. We aren't really committed to each other as persons and there isn't much depth of mutual concern. If one of my 'co-workers' were to die or move to Africa, would I be sad? Probably not, because we haven't truly been friends. Only the work mattered.

A New Testament pattern

'We loved you so much that we were delighted to share with you not only the gospel of God but our lives as well, because you had become *so dear to us*' (1 Thessalonians 2:8).

Paul's joy in Thessalonica was not just the preaching of the gospel but the friendships he had. He preached the good news because he loved them.

Why did Paul want Timothy to visit him in prison? Did he merely want to receive the books and his winter coat? No, he wanted to see Timothy just for the joy of being with him.

Jesus Himself was more than a master, teacher and co-worker in his relationship with the disciples and others. He truly thought of them as friends, (John 15:15) and he really enjoyed being with them.

Getting Our Priorities Right

Yes, I've suggested that people matter more than projects. That doesn't mean I believe Christians shouldn't be active in their service for God. Far from it, I'm a very busy person myself being involved in teaching, administration and counselling. My concern is that we should each get our priorities right. Most of us have placed work ahead of people. We tend to feel satisfied when the team project is a success regardless of what's happened to us as people. Our efforts have been put into the job rather than into first building up loving relationships among team members.

'Productivity, efficiency, percentages, bonuses...' these are todays 'in' words. People don't seem to matter. Something of this attitude has spilled over into Church life. We may not actually say so but we often feel that time spent with each other just for the sake of fellowship is *wasted* time. There is no end product like a soul won or a meeting organised. We can't easily measure the benefits of putting efforts into friendships, and so we focus our attention on activities which produce definite results.

Trying a new lifestyle

There are two reasons why I used to put activities before fellowship. The first was ignorance. The second was fear. My eagerness to throw my whole weight into Christian service was a form of escape. The truth is that I was scared to enter into close relationships. I always got on well with people but that was as far as I dared to go. So I decided that getting to know people was a waste of time. Now I really want to know people and to love and be loved. My priorities have changed.

It hasn't been easy to rearrange my time in order to put Christians before service. I've faced some criticism too. It's meant resigning from several committees and cutting down the number of preaching engagements I accept. Most of my time is spent caring for the well-being of other people but I've also learnt to put myself high on my priority list. I realise that my own body, soul and spirit need nourishment.

God wants a healthy servant not an emotional, physical and spiritual wreck.

To take care of myself I set aside time which no one can touch except in an emergency. Recently I went away for a whole week by myself to recharge my batteries before facing a busy term at college.

In everyday life, most of my relationships involve nothing but giving out so I am especially thankful for a small group of close friends who are prepared to meet my needs and whom I can build up and encourage in return. These friendships are very precious. We often pray together when we're free, or talk on the phone, or simply enjoy times of relaxed fellowship.

Some readers may feel as I did about closeness—it's unnecessary and a waste of time. You'd rather be doing something. This is often why the quality of church life is so poor. Most of us aren't ready to try a new life style. We can be just the same with Jesus—always rushing about serving him (like Martha) when often he'd prefer to talk to us quietly. I agree that there's a great deal to be done, but we shall be far more effective in our Christian service if first we give time to each other.

How Close Should We Be?

I've mentioned that some of my closest friends and I are committed to each other. So what do I mean by 'committed'.

The most committed relationship I have is with Nancy, because I'm married to her. We've learned that love's more than just a sentimental feeling when we see each other. It's something active and commits us to love, work and care for one another. There's no escape from the duties we have towards each other. Even when there's a really rough patch we can't run away and pretend the relationship doesn't exist. We simply have to find a solution because the marriage vows cover both the good times and the bad ones.

Many young people are not prepared to get married because of the price they might have to pay later—so they just live together instead. If it doesn't work they simply split up. Others get married but when there are serious problems to sort out, they won't make the effort to solve them and so they get divorced. Their commitment has strings attached to it—they'll stay together so long as things are easy and happy.

The meaning of commitment

'But surely a marriage commitment is very different from Christian relationships. We're not married to each other, we just attend the same church' you might say.

There are many differences but there are also some important similarities. When a young man goes to the altar, he marries into his fiancée's family. Whether he likes it or not his wife's relations become his too. Only after marriage does he fully realise in practice the need to relate to his new parents, uncles, aunts, brothers and sisters. In a sense, when we gave our lives to Christ we also committed ourselves to the members of his Church. We are each part of God's family, the body of Christ. Like the young bridegroom, few of us had any idea what it would mean to be brought into a new family.

It's very easy to agree intellectually with the doctrine of the body of Christ. Only later do we discover that it involves real people, and that they're here to stay. We realise they are not all nice, interesting, talented people (like ourselves!). For some of us it's fairly easy to be dedicated to God, but it's much harder to share our lives with other people (some of whom we don't really like).

The truth that commitment already exists between us is even more startling when we think about Paul's teaching in 1 Corinthians 12:14. He says Christians are like the different parts of a human body. These are physically connected to each other and have to help each other if the body is to work properly. My knee can't decide to opt out if it decides it doesn't like my foot—the two are so closely linked that they must work together happily. God isn't asking us to make a decision as to whether we should be linked to each other—he is telling us that we *are* joined together and that we should act as if we were.

God expects us to share ourselves much more deeply than

we do now. Obviously some parts of our lives ought to stay private. Other areas should be open. It's more than just friendliness or what is the 'done thing' socially. It's making a love commitment to each other as Christ did to his disciples. He'd like me to be able to say to you: 'I love you. I'm glad you're my brother in Christ. When you need me I'll be there and you can depend on me not to pull out when things get tough.'

'I want to'

Some marriages are cold and miserable. The couples fulfil only what is legally required to stay married. Others are active and joyful love affairs. The same kind of difference exists in Christian relationships too. Many believers agree in their heads that they are members one of another, but it goes no further than that. Their contact with other Christians is insincere and shallow. A growing number of Christians see that we must live up to our theology—and that means building up active, caring friendships.

I used to try to love people because I felt I ought to. I was never very successful because of my own fears and inability to get close to people. I used to feel guilty and frustrated. It was a failure. Here was I, a Christian leader, unable and to some extent unwilling to fulfil the command to love. Then God started changing my attitudes from a cold 'I ought to' to a much warmer 'I want to.'

I am slowly realising that deeper friendships are meant to exist outside my own family circle. This includes singles, marrieds, old and young, men and women. I want people to be able to say more than—'Fine thank you', when I ask them how they are. We are very unused to such honesty and openness. Sometimes I have to ask a person several times before he says how he really feels. More than once I've tried to answer the question, 'How are you?' truthfully. To my horror the person who said it disappeared before I had fully replied because nothing more than a polite answer was expected from me.

One or two men who have attempted land and water speed records have refused an ejector button in their cabs—they wanted to remain committed to the task, whatever the danger. They were literally prepared to lay down their lives. We are to do the same for each other, and occasionally it will mean actual death. More often it means not pressing the escape button when a friendship is costing me too much. It could mean being hurt and rejected by someone when I've allowed myself to become close. It could mean staying up half the night with someone who may need my help. This is what commitment is all about.

What turned the frog into a prince?

There is a touching children's story called 'The Princess and the Frog.' A young princess by accident dropped her favourite toy—a golden ball—into a pool of water. A frog said that he'd dive in after it but he wanted a reward on his return. The princess said that he could have anything he liked—her clothes, her jewels or even her golden crown.

This is how he replied:

'I do not want your clothes or your jewels or even your golden crown. I should like you to love me. I want you to let me be your friend and play with you. I want to sit beside you at the table, eat from your golden plate and drink from your golden cup. I want to sleep in your bed beside you.'

What did the slimy green frog want most of all? Not material things, but love, friendship and acceptance by a beautiful princess. But when he found the ball for her, the girl broke her promise. The poor frog was really upset. The father of the princess forced her to fulfil her vow, but she didn't do it willingly or happily. In the end the frog turned into a handsome prince. And only when he'd changed into a fine young man did she love and marry him.

When I was a teenager I felt like that poor frog. I badly needed relationships in which I was loved and accepted as I was. That would have helped me to become a more loving person. I was so depserate that I'd have accepted the friendship of anyone. Fortunately that 'anyone' turned out to be Christ. I soon joined a church, and I found that the people there actually seemed to like me. Two families opened their hearts and homes to me. I could come and go as I pleased. They loved me as if I were their own son. I was so broken that for a long time I could offer nothing in return, but it didn't seem to matter to them. They just kept on loving me. For the first time in my life I knew I was accepted.

Accept Me As I Am

Once at a conference in the Midlands, I found myself listening to a person who needed counselling. I began correctly by allowing her to talk while I said nothing. Then I started to think about my own burdens rather than hers. The conversation changed direction. She was forced to listen to me. She became quite distressed and said, 'It always happens like this. I want to talk about my problems and it ends up with me hearing someone else's instead.'

What she'd said was true and it shocked me. I was following my usual pattern of being self-centred. But the time had come for me to help her in the same way as my friends had cared for me when I was a teenager. This time I listened without interruption, seeking nothing for myself. Soon, as I listened to her, she began to feel a sense of security and genuine love.

'Am I allowed to cry?' she asked.

'Of course you are,' I replied.

Then she wept freely. Why I wondered, did she have to ask my permission to cry? I discovered that crying was unacceptable to her closest friends. Their love for her had conditions attached to it, and 'not crying' was one of them. What she needed was to be accepted just as she was, and at that moment I became the kind of friend she needed. It changed her and it changed me. I have not been the same since. Some time later she gave me a poster: on the back she had written: 'Thank you for the love, care, prayer and understanding we have shared in Christ.'

Giving and receiving

The princess loved and accepted the frog only when he turned into a handsome prince. We often behave like this—we'll love people provided they become what we want them to be. Our acceptance has strings attached. Most Christians can't turn into princes for my benefit. Like the frog they feel depressed, unloved, ignored and rejected. Some try to be the kind of people others will like by acting out the part. It doesn't work because in the end they know that they are not accepted for who they really are.

It was touching to receive a letter from a missionary who wrote, 'Thank you for being you.' Here was somebody who had learned how to love people without demanding that they change first. She allowed individuals to be themselves. It's a wonderful experience to be with someone like that. You can simply relax and be yourself. No play-acting or pretending is needed.

God wants this kind of atmosphere in the church—each of us free to be ourselves without fear of rejection. He wants to see a quality of love that doesn't exist in society. This will help to mend the broken hearts of those who've been hurt in life. They'll begin to live and grow and I did.

It's tempting to sit back and say, '*They* should be loving and accepting *me* because I've had a hard life and I need it.' If everyone felt that, nothing would happen. We'd all be waiting for someone else to make the first move. So why don't I take the initiative in my church?

I may fear being utterly drained of love, receiving nothing in return. Sometimes it's a bit like that at first. But as other people benefit from my love and care, they'll begin to do the same for me. The apostle Paul was always in danger of having one-sided relationships and yet he could still write of 'giving *and* receiving (Philippians 4:15) in his fellowship with the Philippian church. Only as each of us loves and is loved will the church begin to grow.

> From him (i.c. Christ) the whole body (i.e. the church)...grows and builds itself up in love, as each part does its work' (Ephesians 4:16).

Points to Ponder

1. Has reading this chapter changed your idea of Christian fellowship? If it has, in what ways?

2. How real do you think is the danger of trusting in people rather than in God?

3. Think of some church activity you are involved in. If it suddenly ended, what would be left of your relationship with the people you have been working with?

4. Is time spent with others just for the sake of fellowship wasted time? How much time do you personally spend just being with people?

5. Jesus had genuine friendships with his disciples and others. How should this fact affect my attitude to close relationships?

6. How do you react to the fact that simply because you are a Christian you have a whole set of Christian 'relations'?

7. Are individuals in your fellowship really committed to each other?

8. To what degree do you feel that you accept people unconditionally?

9. What could be done in your fellowship to encourage individuals to grow closer together?

"...OTHER HELPERS COME ALONG AND SHE'S NO LONGER NEEDED, AND BECOMES ANGRY AND HURT.

11

Giving and Receiving
Derek

Satan wandered into a church one Sunday morning. A sidesman greeted him, handed him a hymn book and pointed to a wide selection of empty places from which he could choose to sit. He headed for a seat near the back so that he could observe the people he'd been working on for several years. As he looked around, a smile of deep satisfaction spread across his face—there were very few backsliders.

By the time the service was due to begin the church was half-full so that most people were able to sit by themselves. Mr Loner, who arrived rather later than usual, almost had to join someone, but at the last minute he found a vacant spot in the front row. For years he had made it his policy to depend on God alone and never accept help or encouragement from people. Much further along his row was Mrs Self-denial who felt compelled continually to give everything away. She looked a mess in her shabby out-of-date clothes. Her generosity was anything but joyful—she did it because God always seemed to be getting at her and making her feel constantly guilty.

Her father, Mr Mean, was quite a wealthy man and could easily have given a tenth of his income to God, but he didn't see why he should, especially as others weren't pulling their weight. However, he made sure that his five pound note was clearly seen by others as he slowly stuffed it into the collection bag.

Further back, Mrs Cling had sandwiched herself between two other ladies. She couldn't bear to sit alone. The trouble was that no one really wanted her company because she pestered the life out of everyone by constantly referring to her problems. She clung like a leech to anyone who'd listen.

Nineteen-year-old Roger Grudge, in his usual back row seat, was being his normal miserable self. He had plenty of time to spare, and some useful talents, but he never did anything for anyone. He wasn't going to help people who never helped him.

In the middle of the church, elderly Mrs Sad gazed blankly ahead of her. She hated sitting alone but hadn't the courage to do anything about it, because she felt that no one liked her. She had far more to cope with than Mrs Cling but she didn't want to put people to any trouble. One or two had tried to offer help but she had declined.

Satan was greatly encouraged by what he saw. What particularly delighted him was the stampede for the door the moment the service had finished—it made absolutely sure that there would be no opportunity for the Christians to love and care for each other than morning. He wouldn't need to visit that church again for quite a while....

It happens too often

Situations like this are all too common. What's missing is the 'giving and receiving' which Paul wrote about in his letter to the Philippian Church (Philippians 4:15). It isn't merely a problem found in half-empty churches either. Sometimes I preach in tiny chapels where the people are jammed in like sardines. You'd think such closeness would guarantee mutual care and concern, but it doesn't. You can be as distant from someone almost sitting on your lap as you are from a person who is eight rows away.

Fellowship involves a two-way process. Each of us gives and therefore each receives. A church has no real life if its members are not relating to each other in this way. It's essentially dead. How can people grow if others are unwilling to give them the help they need to develop? How can those with problems get them sorted out if they won't allow their friends to get near them? How can the pastor look after sixty people properly when two or three selfishly take up all his time and energy? How can missionary work be supported when only a few are willing to tithe their incomes?

A good proportion of our church members are neither giving nor receiving. They drift in and out of church when they feel like it. They're like people who claim to support their local football club yet only turn up to watch them play once a year. Sometimes those who are involved are unbalanced in their attitudes and actions. Some spend all their time giving out. Others do nothing but take in, without giving a thought to those whom they might help.

Let's look at some of the reasons why we have so many problems with giving.

Problems with Giving

No money

'It's easy for rich Christians to give a tenth of their income to God. But how can I be expected to do the same? If I creamed off a tithe every week I wouldn't be able to pay my bills or keep up the mortgage payments.'

This is the kind of excuse I'd used for years. To be honest, I'd always been mean with money, even as a child. When I became a Christian I stayed mean. I simply couldn't trust God to provide for me if I took the risk of being generous.

No time

'My job isn't the nine to five type. I have to work all hours. I'd love to give more time to serving the church but I do need to relax sometimes, and that uses up what free time I have.'

Priorities between work, family life and church are very difficult to work out. Some neglect their wives and children for the church. A few allow their work to suffer for the sake of their Christian service. Too many, however, make work and family life an excuse for not bothering to serve God in their local church.

No use

'I'd love to teach in Junior Church or visit the sick, but God has made me one of those people who contribute best by just attending services and staying in the background. Being active isn't really my scene.'

For some, this is a genuine problem—they really believe that God has not equipped them to do anything useful. That's untrue, as we read in 1 Corinthians 12. For others, it's simply a lame excuse because they don't want to pull their weight.

As a duty

Some Christians only give when they're forced to by God, or when people put pressure on them. It's a sad kind of giving that's driven along only by a voice shouting, 'You must give, you must give!' True, we are commanded in the Bible to give, yet if our talents and money are grudgingly offered, there's little satisfaction for us or those who receive from us.

Guilt and anger used to well up inside me whenever I heard the expression 'the joy of giving.' I felt no joy and I never gave more than the bare minimum. Mary, on the other hand, gave practically all her money away, but she had no joy either. She was made to do it by the idea of a God who hounded her with verses like, 'It is more blessed to give than to receive' (Acts 20:35).

Christian giving should be a matter of love rather than duty: as Paul put it in 1 Corinthians 13:3 'If I give all I possess to the poor...but have not love, I gain nothing.'

To gain admiration

I've always given a great deal of time to those who needed teaching or counselling. Much of it was in effect no more than an ego trip. I wanted to be admired and known as someone who cared. I did much of it to satisfy my own feelings rather than out of concern for the well-being of others. Mary's generosity with money was always done 'anonymously' yet somehow everyone knew about it. Secretly, she wanted her heroic self-sacrifice to be widely known and to gain a good reputation among her friends and with God.

To settle accounts

Most of us tend to work on this basis at one time or another. A young mum may say to herself, 'I'd better bring Joan's kids home from school today because she did it for me last week!' Or I may buy someone a Christmas present because he gave me one last year. It's part of our upbringing to return kindness for kindness. There's nothing wrong in that, but if the only reason I'm helpful is because someone has done me a favour, then a sense of obligation rather than love controls my life.

To meet my own needs

It's quite natural to feel fulfilled when someone needs me, because my God-given abilities are meant to be used in helping people. But what motivates me? Do I help him because I really love him? Or is it mainly for my benefit so that my needs can be met by having someone dependent on me?

Sometimes I have to examine carefully my reasons for counselling people. I find that when the person I'm trying to help no longer needs me, I feel useless and hollow inside. It's the same when someone I'm counselling suddenly decides to go to a colleague instead of me. I feel undervalued and hurt. It can happen to any of us. For example, a lady may have been serving tea at the annual church meeting for many years. As time goes by other helpers come along and she's no longer needed, and becomes angry and hurt. But why was she doing it in the first place?

Yes, the need to be needed is perfectly normal. Yet if it controls what I do, I should ask God to change my attitude so that I'll serve others because I truly care for them.

What the Bible Says About Giving

Some Christians see God as someone whose main aim is *to make life miserable* for them. He's someone who always wants to rob them of their energies and money against their wills. So what do they do? They rebel against him and lock away their talents and treasures as if from a burglar. They turn in on themselves and rarely have much consideration for the needs of others. They may consent to giving a little bit away but it's done grudgingly in a loveless, joyless manner.

But God isn't like that at all. He doesn't want to wrench good things out of our hands. He wants to load us up with better things, 'The thief comes only to steal and kill and destroy; I have come that they may have life, and have it to the full' (John 10:10). But so long as we're holding him back by clinging to what he gives us, he's unable to pour greater riches into our laps. 'If you have not been trustworthy in handling wordly wealth, who will trust you with true riches?' (Luke 16:11).

Then there are those who are *taken up by all the Scriptures which refer to self-denial*. 'If anyone would come after me (Jesus), he must deny himself and take up his cross and follow me' (Mark 8:34). Such people almost 'drive themselves into the ground' trying to obey them. They look hard at teaching like, 'If anyone has material possessions and sees his brother in need but has no pity on him, how can the love of God be in him?' (1 John 3:17), and they feel that any money or goods they have should be given away. A Christian who thinks this way will always appear to be other-centred and he'll have little concern for his own needs. He probably won't question much his motive for giving, he'll just give because God says he should. But there'll be little love or joy involved when he does it.

But God doesn't just want me to love others, he wants me to love me: 'Love your neighbour *as yourself*' (Matthew 19:19). Before I can love others properly I must learn how to accept and love myself as God does. If I beat myself over the head with verses about self-denial I'm not loving myself and God will not be glorified if I feel constantly guilty if I do anything solely for my own pleasure. He wants me to enjoy life, not to endure it!

Not rules—but following Jesus

The Bible does not teach self-denial as a set of rules. It means quite simply that I must do what God wants on each occasion. Sometimes I may need to sacrifice an evening's leisure or give away a hundred pounds. On other occasions I should relax at home or buy myself a new coat. Self-denial often does hurt, but I shouldn't feel guilty if God's will and mine are the same and there's no suffering involved. Following Jesus doesn't mean hardship *all* the time! It can be enjoyable too!

Jesus wants us to be like him in our giving. Now he didn't give his all to people because it was just his duty, or to gain their admiration. He gave because he really loved them. Why did he love them so much? It was because he was filled with his Father's love. 'As the Father has loved me, so have I loved you' (John 15:9). That deep spring of love overflowed onto mankind and Jesus joyfully became a servant, and finally laid down his life for His people.

After Jesus had said, '...so have I loved you,' he added, 'Now remain in my love.' When we allow the love of God to penetrate our icy human hearts, it melts away the hardness and transforms our attitudes to him and to our fellow Christians.

Mary had an ogre God, I had a mean God. As the gentle warmth of his love flowed into our lives, God seemed to change, and the 'I ought' became 'I want' to give to others.

Mary is no longer obsessed with giving all her money away. She still gives generously but she does it freely and happily. She's even bought herself some attractive clothes because she's suddenly discovered that she needs to love herself just as God does.

My attitude to money has changed dramatically. Not long ago, when I was unexpectedly given several hundred pounds, instead of hanging on to it, I simply gave it away with no regrets. I still give hours of my time to counselling but it's because I love people that I now do it. I'm still pleased when someone compliments me but it's not man's praise that does all the driving—it's the love of God filling my heart.

Receiving

'You'd think that receiving would be a simple matter, with no problems. Don't you believe it! Some people can't (or won't) accept help and love. Others do receive but for the wrong reasons. Perhaps our response is—'I can manage on my own thank you.'

I can manage on my own

'Independence' is the key word. It's a sad response because it robs both the receiver of the love and support which he needs, and the giver of the happiness of expressing his concern. This was Mary's attitude. She really hated having to depend on anyone else but herself, and (as she put it) 'on the Lord.'

It's true that we ought not to 'cling' but some people are independent to the extent of living in their own private worlds and not letting anyone else in.

I must pay you back

When you were a child you were probably told, 'It's greedy and selfish to receive something unless you can return the kindness.' We grow up with the idea that it's wrong to accept gifts and time unless we can somehow repay. When we do finally allow a person to help us, we immediately search for some way of returning that generosity.

When we develop a wrong sense of guilt about receiving, it cuts us off from God as well as from people. We can only partially accept his love, care, time and forgiveness because of this feeling that it ought to be earned before we dare receive it. Mary found this in her prayer life—she felt she only deserved God's blessing after spending ages on her knees each day.

A few Christmases ago, Mary stayed with us for several weeks (rather than going home to London), so that she could be involved in church activities. She tried to get a job but there were none available, so she had no money to offer Nancy towards her housekeeping costs. That made Mary very unhappy because she was forced to receive with no possibility of repaying. This was all wrong, according to her standards.

I'm not worth helping

Some folks don't want to put people out because of their own low self-esteem. They feel, 'I'm not good enough'; or, 'People don't really love me; they're just sorry for me.' They don't feel deserving enough to accept someone else's time and effort. It makes them guilty so they avoid it, thus losing out themselves as well as robbing those who wish to help of the joy of doing so.

Mary was like this at college. She always thought I was too busy to see her and hated taking up my 'valuable' time. When we prayed she never volunteered to have her own needs mentioned—it always had to be someone else's. She didn't feel important enough to let somebody else tell God what bothered her.

We often think that God has an unloving attitude to us. I remember one Christian who admitted that she didn't really know whether God loved her. It wasn't lack of Bible knowledge that stopped her from enjoying God's love, it was her damaged emotions. She just couldn't believe in her heart that she had any value in God's eyes.

Give me...give me!

Some people are eager to receive because they're selfish and greedy. They get what they can out of their friends. I was a real money grabber and I held onto what I had. I may have had a reasonable excuse when I was poor, but when better days came along things didn't change. I remained a Scrooge.

It was the same emotionally. I drained people dry. It's true that I did need a lot of help in my teens and early twenties, but I never considered the feelings of those who were kind to me.

Not for me

We return to Mary's testimony again. She was happy to accept gifts of money, so long as it was for college fees or car repairs—that is 'impersonal' things. She had a real hang-up about being given luxuries for herself or spending money for her own pleasure. She kept her clothes until they were too frayed to wear. One pair of shoes literally fell apart at the seams before they were consigned to the dustbin. Friends had to think hard what birthday presents to give her because they feared she'd give them away again.

If it gives you pleasure

Some people feel really guilty if they get pleasure from having something done for them. So they block off their pleasure and accept help only because of the joy it brings to the giver.

What The Bible Says About Recieving

Scripture gives us the real picture of God. He is not mean nor do his favours have to be earned. He has already given his Son for us (John 3:16) and at some time in the past we decided once for all to receive him into our lives (John 1:12). It didn't finish there because the same God who gave us Jesus is continually providing for us. 'He who did not spare his own Son...how will he not also, along with him graciously give us all things?' (Romans 8:32). If his outstretched hands are offering heaven's riches, who am I to refuse them?

God has brought us into a new family, the Church, through which he builds us up. When we became Christians, God could have made us so that we would depend on him alone, but he decided not to. He wants to nourish us through fellowship, teaching, prayer, care and provision of practical needs. He wants me to be willing to accept what he provides through others.

Was Jesus a giver or a receiver? He was both. We all know about his activities as a giver, but to what extent did he receive?

One thing is certain—Jesus could easily have managed without help from any human being, but he chose not to. He could have turned stones into bread but he invited himself into people's homes for food and hospitality. As far as we know he never paid for what he was given. He allowed people to show human affection towards him— like the woman who spread the precious ointment over his feet and shed tears over them. He wanted the close friendship and support of his disciples on the night he was betrayed.

Jesus, even though he was God, wanted to receive from his friends. How much more we need to do the same.

When we find out what God is really like, we are able to accept from him the benefits he wants to shower on us. 'How much more will your Father in heaven give good gifts to those who ask him! (Matthew 7:11). He may want to meet our needs himself or he may want to do it through other Christians.

When Mary realised that God wanted to give to her through her friends, it was a great discovery. It allowed her to appreciate the genuine concern which people had been striving to show her, and it unlocked the door to the enjoyment of God's love. Her relationship with God is much more relaxed because she now knows that he's smiling and stretching out his hands to her. He's also showing her that it's not wrong to allow people to come alongside in times of joy or sorrow. Mary now enjoys her God-given humanity and sees it not as a weakness but as an essential part of her. She allows people to pray about her needs as well as theirs.

So Where Are You?

Are you too heavily dependent on people—a receiver only? Or are you cold, isolated and independent? Do you know God loves you, or is his love conditional upon your efforts? Do you give everything away on principle? Or do you grab and hoard in case a rainy day comes along? Can God be trusted to supply your needs if you are generous?

Like pendulums we have swung one way or the other. Not everyone will be as unbalanced as Mary and I were, but each of us has room for improvements somewhere. What God asks is a willingness to examine ourselves and to allow him to correct us so that we'll help each other to grow as we give and receive.

At last, the joy of giving and receiving

When I discover the real God, I find that he accepts me as I am and that his love for me has no strings attached to it. In that atmosphere of love, he often gives me commands which involve self-sacrifice. He doesn't do it to make me unhappy but because he wants to use me to benefit others. Only when I know his love will I have joy in doing what he asks. When he commands me to give, I'll never be the loser, even though human calculations often tell me that I will. He doesn't promise to repay in exactly the same way, but because I have freely given, he will freely reward in his own way. 'Give, and it will be given to you. A good measure, pressed down, shaken together and running over, will be poured into your lap. For with the measure you use, it will be measured to you' (Luke 6:38).

When I allow myself to receive from God my attitude to myself changes. Instead of thinking, 'I'm a useless nobody', I can say, 'I'm a somebody because God says so,' (Matthew 6:25-27). Now that I know I'm a somebody, I can receive from God's children without apology. However, he doesn't want me to drain them dry, but to accept love, care and money when I need them. Under these circumstances it's not shameful to be a receiver, but is God's will, and brings joy to the giver.

Recently I received the most beautiful Christmas card I can ever remember. It wasn't a huge card, just a tiny one measuring 2½" x 4". On the front was a robin sitting on a spade. Inside were the words: 'Thank you for giving me so much of Jesus.'

It was from a teenager. I was deeply moved by that card because I'd no idea that I'd given her so much. I thought the reverse was true—she had given and I had received. Because I'm a leader, very few people ask me how I am or how things are going at college—but she had often done this and I appreciated her genuine love for me.

Somehow, without either of us being aware of it, we had

both given and received. Neither of us felt any obligation or great sacrifice in doing so. It was quite natural. It's just a simple illustration of what should be happening throughout each church regardless of age, sex or position. Today I may give, tomorrow I may receive. Next Sunday I may do both. This gentle ebbing and flowing of Christian love is God's plan for his Church.

Points to Ponder

1. Think about yourself for a moment. Are you like any of the people mentioned in this chapter: Mr. Loner, Mrs. Self-denial, Mr. Mean, Mrs. Cling, Roger Grudge or Mrs. Sad?

2. What are the things that prevent you from giving more than you do? ('I'm useless... too busy... too poor...') How valid are these excuses?

3. What motivates you to give? Is it a sense of duty, a desire to be admired, the fact that someone has given to you first, your own need to be needed? Are there any other reasons?

4. Do you feel that God always wants to grab what you've got? If so, do you find yourself clinging to things to prevent him from getting at them?

5. Do you usually feel compelled to give away any gift you receive because you feel that God doesn't want you to keep things for yourself?

6. Do you find it difficult to receive? How often do you say, 'I can manage alone,' or, 'Only if I can give something to you!' How often do you think, 'I'm not worth helping?'

7. How do you receive from others? Do you grasp what you can, receive to spend on others, receive to keep the giver happy? Are there any other ways?

8. Are you prepared to receive from God through your Christian friends or do you feel this is wrong? If your Christian friends want to give to you, do you receive the gift as coming from God? Or do you feel uneasy?

9. Are you personally balanced in your giving and receiving? If not, how could you improve the balance?

10. How can you help others in your fellowship to be better givers and receivers?

" AN UNEXPECTED GIFT OF SOAP, CAKES OR
FLOWERS (OR EVEN SOME CABBAGE PLANTS)
IS ENCOURAGING. "

12

All Aboard
Derek

Well, have you made up your mind yet? Do you really want to be open with other people? Are you prepared to get involved in deep relationships? Are you willing to experience new joy in giving and receiving? It's only when you're happy to let God into these areas that you can participate effectively in the ongoing life of the church.

There's nothing I can do

When you look around your church, do you feel jealous of all the gifted people who are continually doing wonderful things for God? Mrs Crabtree has a constant stream of women visiting her home for counselling. John Parker is only in his mid-twenties, but is a great preacher already. Then there's Freda Jones who always seems to be surrounded by children who want to talk about Jesus... Bernard Johnson who gives such clear exposition of Scripture each week...Christine Rowlands who prays so beautifully in public.

Thousands of Christians seem to be happily attending church services week by week. At least they look happy on the outside. On the inside, it's a very different story—they feel useless and unwanted. The more others shine, the worse they feel. St Paul discovered that some people in the Corinthian church had exactly the same problem. A few of them felt so miserable that they even said 'I do not belong to the body' (1 Corinthians 12:16). With so many talented people using their gifts in public, the quieter ones thought that God had forgotten to equip them to do anything.

Are you one of these left-out people? No one seems to notice you, or ask you to do anything. You feel a great admiration for the clever people. Yet it is mixed with jealousy and even hostility. You daren't offer your help in case it's rejected. So you just battle on alone. You don't seem to belong. No one seems to care, not even God.

Good news

I have good news for you! Even if no one else notices you, God cares, and he doesn't want you to be left out! When you became a Christian, God did more than just bring salvation to you as an individual, leaving you to struggle alone until you reached heaven. He placed you in his Church, which the Bible calls the Body of Christ. Every believer belongs to this body. 'We were *all* baptised by one Spirit into one Body—whether Jews or Greeks, slaves or free—and we were *all* given the one Spirit to drink' (1 Corinthians 12:13).

That's not the end of the good news. God gave the same powerful Holy Spirit to each Christian. Yes, to you as well as Mrs Crabtree and Bernard Johnson. The Holy Spirit does some wonderful things for us. By enabling each of us to participate in a vital and unique way he makes sure that we're not left out of the active life of the church. 'To each one the manifestation of the Spirit is given for the common good' (1 Corinthians 12:7).

What would you say if I told you that your church couldn't do without your contribution to its life? 'Rubbish!' you might reply. 'Anything I can do is too small to be of any real value.' Wrong! Read Paul's encouraging words: 'Those parts of the body that seem to be weaker are indispensable, and the parts that we think are less honourable we treat with special honour' (1 Corinithians 12:22f). These verses are speaking to you. Do you believe this? Because if you did your life, and that of your church, would be changed.

Unfortunately, a number of churches are not encouraging all their members to be useful. Some people are being ignored completely. They have valuable gifts to contribute but are being stifled by pastors who feel threatened and want to do everything themselves.

Think of your body for a moment. It works properly only when all the organs are healthy. When one part is diseased or not functioning properly, the rest of you suffers. When you have a throbbing bruise on your leg, you can't concentrate on work. If you have a stomach upset, you become irritable.

Your church is like your body—every member is needed. 'The whole body...grows and builds itself up in love, as *each part* does its work' (Ephesians 4:16). *Each part* is essential and must be doing what God wants it to do. You may think of yourself as only 'weak' or 'less honourable'—but, praise God, it's people like you whom God needs most (I didn't say this, Paul did!) So don't worry about the abilities which others possess, just concentrate on what you can do to help your church to grow and stay healthy.

Love—most important of all

What's the most important task you can do in your church? It's not which task you can do that really matters but whether you love people. Paul placed love higher on the list than all the marvellous spiritual gifts available to us. Of course, gifts are essential in the church, that's why Paul wrote three lists of them in his epistles. He wanted every Christian to use whatever ability God had given him. But most of all he desired a loving attitude among Christians. Without love, even dying for the Christian faith is not worth much. The same applies to the working of miracles through prayer. However spectacular the release of such power may be, a miracle worker is a nobody if his heart is loveless and cold.

We should certainly pray about which particular gifts God wants us to have, so that the whole church may benefit. But we don't need to pray about whether or not we should love our fellow believers. Each of us is meant to participate in church life by sharing love, regardless of which special abilities we may have. The command to 'build each other up' (1 Thessalonians 5:11), is written to all Christians, that is to you and me. None of us is allowed to opt out. Real growth can take place only in a loving atmosphere, and this is created when each individual is playing his or her part.

"I've tried to be loving but I can't."

I've been told this a hundred times by Christians who dearly want to be more loving in their attitudes and actions. They see others radiating warmth and affection and it makes them feel frustrated and guilty. Is this your experience? Would you like to be different? There are two steps you can take.

First, make sure that you are really close to Jesus. Sometimes barriers have to be removed to make that possible.

Second, ask Jesus for a new infilling of his love.

'If our hearts do not condemn us...(we) receive from him anything we ask' (1 John 3:21f). First, we must realise that it is *from Christ* that the body builds itself up in love (Ephesians 4:16). He is the source of my love for others. If anything blocks the channel of his love flowing to me, then I shall have neither the desire nor the ability to care for my fellow Christians. It's as simple as that. There will be no 'rivers of living water' flowing from me because there won't be any flowing into me. My life will be like the British reservoirs during the great drought—ninety per cent empty and often stagnant.

Confession and obedience

In his epistle, John states that there can be a loving concern for others only when our relationship with Christ is healthy. 'Whoever loves his brother lives in the light' (1 John 2:10). God's light exposes our sins and we feel condemned and guilty, until we confess them and accept his forgiveness. That knowledge and experience of forgiveness sets us free to forgive others and to begin to love them.

'But if anyone obeys his word, God's love is truly made complete in him' (1 John 2:5). Disobedience blocks the enjoyment of God's love to us. It's like a father and his child. A naughty child constantly earns his father's displeasure, much of whose time is spent punishing and correcting. An obedient child sees a smiling face much more often, and really appreciates his father's love. He will be more relaxed and free and will be more pleasant to his brothers and sisters. It's like that with us and God. When he is happy with our lives, we'll act in more loving ways towards members of our spiritual family.

Secondly, we should realise that 'God's love is poured into our hearts' Romans 5:5). For the first eighteen years of my Christian life, I knew with my mind that God loved me, but my heart had never been touched. I knew in theory that I should love people and I tried desperately to do it but with little success. As far as I can tell I was a hardworking Christian, yet inside me there was a numbing coldness. I felt uncomfortable among those who radiated real love. I rejected them because I could face only a more intellectual approach to caring for people.

So what happened to change things? I don't know exactly. All I know is that the promise in Romans 5:5 that God would pour his love into my heart literally came true. Somewhere inside me an empty hollow began filling up with God's love, until it overflowed to other people. It was a definite experience with nothing academic about it! I could truly say I 'love' because 'he first loved' me (1 John 4:19). And I felt the real impact of his love in a way I had never done before. The rivers of living water began to flow, just as Jesus promised in John 7:38.

Knowing the fulness of God's love isn't reserved for special Christians. God wants all of us to enjoy it. He wants us to ask for it and be transformed by it. Your life could be like the reservoirs in the autumn of 1976 which filled with precious rain until they could supply the towns and villages again.

Your infilling will change your whole way of life and you'll be able to nourish others in the church as you reach out to them in love. Instead of a heavy 'I ought' there will be a joyful 'I want' to show love to people.

Love in action

What did God do to show that he truly loved the human race? 'This is how God showed his love among us: he sent his one and only Son into the world...' (1 John 4:9). The answer is: He did something definite. Many Christians think of love as nothing more than having a good feeling about people. But love is much more than that. Jesus set us an example to follow. He didn't just drift around having pleasant thoughts about the world. He deliberately searched for those who needed help. Sometimes he did so much that he became tired and needed a rest. He finally paid the highest price that love can pay by going to the Cross. That was the ultimate proof of his deep concern. 'This is how we know what love is: Jesus Christ laid down his life for us' (1 John 3:16).

So what are we to do? The same as he did, according to St John: 'And we ought to lay down our lives for our brothers' (1 John 3:16). Some Christians will have to fulfil this command literally by losing their lives. Those of us who are unlikely to do this mustn't feel complacent about it. The command applies to each of us, whether we live or die. It means being willing to pay any price God asks as an expression of loving concern.

What might the price be? It could be time, money, patience, practical help, wear and tear on emotions—each given sacrificially for the benefit of someone else. It was not only on the cross that Jesus laid down his life; he did so throughout his life and he calls us to 'follow in his steps' (1 Peter 2:21). We must fulfil what Paul wrote in Romans 15:1-3: 'We (are)... not to please ourselves. Each of us should please his neighbour for his good...For even Christ did not please himself.' So the Bible tells us to be concerned for others—how do we do that?

Loving Attitudes

1. We often forget the importance of *appreciation*.

I know of a man who stole hundreds of pounds from his church because no one appreciated him for what he was doing. The benefits of appreciation are enormous and it costs me very little to make another person feel that I really care about him and his work. I'm not suggesting deliberate flattery—that's wrong and wouldn't help anybody. People need to know that they genuinely matter to us. In an age of criticism we should be looking for things to appreciate in each other. How good we ourselves feel when someone has noticed us and what we're doing.

Society has crushed some people so badly that when they become Christians they still feel unlovable and unwanted. They have lost their self-esteem. Appreciation will help them to recover a right sense of their own value, and they'll be set free to enjoy their Christian lives.

2. We can also show love by *listening*

God gave us two ears but only one mouth! Yet we act as though we were all mouth! Hardly anyone listens any more. Even when we are actually silent during a conversation, our minds are wandering or working out what we want to say next rather than taking in what's being said. Are you prepared to cultivate the art of listening, by thinking deeply about another person's words as he says them? You'll need to reply to his comments, rather than talking immediately about what's on your mind. This may be costly because some people will want you to listen for hours without asking what you think.

3. It helps if we *identify with other people*.

'I wish he knew what it was like to be in my shoes', is a frequent complaint. Yet, if we were truly looking to the interests of others, we should have to reverse our thinking. Paul tells us to feel what others feel and to share in it. 'Rejoice with those who rejoice; mourn with those who mourn' (Romans 12:15). We may not have exactly the same experiences, joys and sorrows but we can try harder to understand what it feels like to be someone else.

One way of identifying with the needs of others is to pray with them about these needs. It not only proves that we care, but it also does something else—it helps them to build up the habit of inviting Jesus into each heartache and joy and it gives them a taste of the value of sharing with a fellow Christian.

4. There is an important ministry of *encouragement*.

Paul writes in 1 Thessalonians 5:14, 'Encourage the timid, help the weak.' In every church there are those who

are fearful and helpless. They never seem to be free from
burdens which are too heavy to bear. Other sad people will
simply have given up because they weren't strong enough to
survive. In his earthly ministry Jesus especially cared for the
broken-hearted and the poor. He loved and strengthened
them so that they could begin to cope with life. He still does
this personally but he often does it through Christians like
you and me.

Labels on boxes containing china often say 'fragile, handle
with care.' That's what God asks us to do for those whose
lives and emotions are delicate or bruised. The Bible says that
we should be gentle, kind, and tender-hearted. Soft and
sentimental? Not a bit of it! It takes courage and effort gently
to help build up those who are in pieces.

'Carry each others' burdens,' says Paul in Galatians 6:2.
'Why can't they give them to Jesus?' you may say. Many
loads are not meant to be given directly to Jesus, they're for
you and me to carry on someone else's behalf. In any case
many areas of help are practical ones, and Jesus isn't here on
earth to do them. But I am and you are. So let's get on with it!

Loving actions

The proof that God's love is in us lies in whether we are
prepared to do things for other people (1 John 3:17).

For instance, every church as poor people in it. Ordinary
church members have needs as well as pastors, evangelists
and missionaries. A friend of mine who is setting up home
was delighted with some left-over bits and pieces from
another church member who was moving to a smaller house.
Paul says of the man who can give, 'Let him give generously'
(Romans 12:8). We don't need to wait until people are in rags
before giving them something. An unexpected gift of soap,
cakes or flowers (or even some cabbage plants) is encouraging.

Loneliness is a sad condition. It affects all ages. One
person I know often takes people out for pizzas, or she visits
those who can't get out. The church is full of lonely people,
even those who have others living in the same house. You can
be lonely in a crowd until someone shows that he cares.

How often to you write letters except to close friends? They are a tremendous encouragement, even if they are just short notes. Think of someone now who would be pleased to hear from you, and drop that person a line. We could use the telephone much more than we do too. We use it a lot for essential calls for business, daily life, or church work, but we could make the extra effort simply to 'make someone happy' as the advertisement puts it.

Have you ever been a young mother going out of her mind after non-stop coping with kids? Or a daughter caring for an aged relative? Or someone not able to get out to do the shopping very easily? These people need help. Christians should be doing something for them.

Upbuilding in love

God expects us to grow. He may want us to help someone else to develop. There are three areas in which we can do it. Each leads naturally onto the next one. First is growth in our relationship with God; second, growth in our relationships with people; third, growth in our usefulness to the Church through Christian service.

1. Close to God

The apostle John knew the reality of God in his life. He wrote his epistles to help to bring others into the deep enjoyment of what he already possessed. 'We proclaim to you what we have seen and heard so that you also may have fellowship with us. And our fellowship is with the Father and his Son, Jesus Christ' (1 John 1:3).

Has Christ become so real you can almost touch him? Then you'll certainly want to share that closeness with anyone who will listen! I am grateful to God for the Christian friends who have taken the trouble to tell me more about Jesus. Without their patience and help I would be a much poorer Christian today.

There are people in your church who'd love to know Jesus better. Who's going to help them, and how are they to do it? Jesus himself will help them. You can do something too. Your life and your words could powerfully influence other Christians. When you radiate the person and love of Christ, people will be attracted to him, and will want to know how they can become closer to him. Some Christians need to know that Jesus cares for them and we can show them that he does by reading the Bible together, talking about him, and praying quietly somewhere.

2. Close to others

Real fellowship with the living God is the basis for loving relationships with his children. The one leads to the other. In spite of this, it's not always automatic. Some aspects of our relationships do fall into place quite naturally without much apparent effort. Others have to be worked at. Using the Bible as our guide we can help one another to learn the secrets of how to relate more happily. Scripture teaches us that before we can build stronger bonds with one another, we have to clear away barriers between us.

No matter how close to God we are, we hurt each other time and time again. When we are mature enough to handle offences against us, and know how to sort out the problems we cause in other people, then we can help others to do the same. None of us likes correcting other people, yet for their own good, and for the sake of the church, we have a responsibility to do it gently and tactfully. Paul writes, 'Teach and admonish one another in all wisdom' (Colossians 3:16).

When we do wrong, it's always against God, and often against another person. So if a relationship has been damaged it must be restored. According to Paul, 'If someone is caught in a sin, you who are spiritual should restore him gently' (Galatians 6:1). Some sins (though not all) are to be confessed openly (James 5:16). Forgiveness is a vital part of relationships and those who are not used to forgiving or being forgiven must be shown its value. We can do this by our example and by our sharing what the Bible says.

Many Christians can't say, 'Sorry', or accept forgiveness from someone else. It may be because they don't know in their own experience that God has forgiven them. When they discover the depth of Christ's love for them in dying to cleanse away their sins that warm appreciation will overflow into forgiveness of other people. Sometimes we should pray with an individual about particular sins which trouble him, together asking God that his love and forgiveness will flood over the offender. This will transform his attitude to those who wrong him.

3. More active service

Some Christians are doing very little for God—they just attend church services. The reasons for inactivity are various. A few are not deeply committed to Christ and his Church and can't be bothered to do anything. They need challenging.!

Others are square pegs in round holes—they work hard but would be better off doing a different task. We can help them to discover their true abilities. I know Christians who are like Timothy was—discouraged and fearful because the going is tough. As Paul did with Timothy, we may be of help in encouraging them to get moving again, urging them to use the gifts which God gave them some time ago.

A final group of belivers might be called the 'sad' people, who feel, 'I'm no good. I have no gifts. I've nothing to offer in my church. I'm useless, no one wants or needs me!' Their need is for sympathetic help because they can do nothing for themselves.

We may begin by gently pointing out that their feelings are going against what God says and that God does have a use for them. But that on its own is not enough. We should explore with them the gifts which they really do have, to see where they fit into the life and service of the church. The next step is to encourage them to take a first step in serving God by performing some small task. The joy of usefulness will lead to further steps and real growth will begin.

It only takes a spark

During the drought of 1976, a team of students was helping the college by working on a series of projects. Their work was hampered by large numbers of hornets zooming about, so they decided to destroy the nest by lighting a small fire round it. A gentle breeze began fanning the flames and the fire soon spread across the dry grass, out of control. Eventually they sent for the fire brigade to prevent damage to the local farmland. The flames were soon put out. We were lucky but other people in the area were less fortunate, and buildings, fields and forests were destroyed by out-of-control fires, each started by a spark or a piece of broken glass.

This is how Christianity spread in the first century. It's no wonder F. F. Bruce chose *The Spreading Flame* as the title for his book on the early church. How did the gospel message spread so fast across the Roman Empire? Through the Church! There was no carefully planned campaign with literature and prayer partners. In some respects it just happened, and no one could stop it. It occurred because the Church was in love with her Lord, and the Christians loved each other. How could such joy be hidden? It couldn't! The flame was so intense within the Church that it burst through into society.

Flame in your life?

Enthusiasm rubs off. Your enjoyment of praise and prayer will attract people. Your delight with the Scriptures will encourage others to try reading their Bibles with a new attitude. Your openness will persuade them to be more open. People will want to spend time with you because you've something worthwhile to share with them. They'll catch fire and in turn will influence others.

You may be the only burning Christian in your church. In six months time there may be two more, and in a year, ten. Some will blossom out overnight, others will move along slowly.

Play-acting masks will be torn off, so that people see each other as they really are, and are then able to love and care more freely. The whole atmosphere will begin to change. A new warmth will replace the old coldness and shallowness, and people will want to be together.

And how about the preacher in Chapter Two? What will

he find. He'll find people who have been in their seats long before he arrives. They'll be preparing themselves for the service. After he announces a hymn or chorus they'll enjoy singing. There'll be an atmosphere of prayer and praise. When the Bible is read publicly, individuals will receive a blessing even before they hear the sermon, because their hearts will be open. When the preacher delivers his message, his prayerful preparation will bear fruit because the congregation will be listening to God's voice and will respond. After it's all over, they'll share together what God has shown them and will express their love for one another in close fellowship.

The process of building itself up in love (Ephesians 4:16), will have begun. Like thousands of others, will you allow God to remove your chains? Will you open up your whole life to Christ and let him set you free? Will you leave behind the dark dungeons of nominal Christianity and come out into his marvellous light? He invites you to do so. Will you accept his offer?

Points to Ponder

1. Does your church have many talented members? In view of this situation, how do you feel about your own contribution?

2. Make a list of the gifts and talents God has given you. To what extent have you offered them to your fellowship?

3. To what extent is love your greatest aim? What does this mean in practice?

4. How difficult do you find it to love other people?

5. Can you think of things in your life which may need sorting out before you can really enjoy God's love? (E.g. some sinful tendency or practice you are unwilling to confess ... some area where you are refusing to obey God...)

6. How far does Romans 5:5 describe your own experience?

7. How important are the following?
   (a) showing appreciation of other people
   (b) listening to what other people say
   (c) bearing their burdens

8. Are we being hypocritical if we express love towards people when we don't have good feelings about them?

9. What practical things do you do for other people? Are there more or different things that you could be doing?

10. How can we help others to be:
    (a) closer to God
    (b) closer to each other
    (c) more active in Christian service?

11. What should a person do if he genuinely feels he is the only 'burning Christian' in his church?